Here For Our Children's Children?

Why we should care for the Earth

Adrian C. Armstrong

imprint-academic.com

Published in the UK by
Imprint Academic, PO Box 200, Exeter EX5 5YX, UK

Published in the USA by
Imprint Academic, Philosophy Documentation Center
PO Box 7147, Charlottesville, VA 22906-7147, USA

ISBN: 9781845401696
A CIP catalogue record for this book is available from the
British Library and US Library of Congress

*Adrian Armstrong is an hydrologist with 30 years practical experience
of water management in agricultural and ecological contexts. He is
honorary professor at Birmingham University, where he lectures in
Environmental Ethics, and is also a priest in the Church of England.*

To my grandchildren Ben and Grace —
it's your world now —
and in memory of Professor John B. Thornes

Contents

Acknowledgements

Here I need to thank all those who have encouraged me to bring this book to completion, and whose ideas and conversations have helped me along the way.

Specifically I would like to thank both Malcolm Clark and my daughter Helen for reading the text; my friends of the Society of Ordained Scientists who have provided so much input over the years; and of course my wife, Margaret, who has both tolerated the work involved, and inspired me to make the effort to do it.

Chapter 1

Introduction

In the film *An Inconvenient Truth*, Al Gore interrupts his exposition of climate change to relate the story of a life-threatening accident to his son. He then explains that this incident showed him how precious human life was, and how much he wanted to preserve the planet for this precious child, and hence for all sons and daughters. In this single section, he opens up the whole issue of environmental ethics, and so seeks to identify and justify his concern for the environment. He introduces this section of the film by saying:

> Ultimately this is really not a political issue so much as a moral issue. If we allow that [i.e. massive rises in atmospheric CO_2] to happen, it is deeply unethical.

His personal response to the question: "why care for the environment?" is then that he values it and wants it to be there for his children. He wants the precious environment to be available to his precious children. His answer is of course only one of the many possible ways that this question can be answered. This book is an attempt to explore the variety of answers to that same single question, but it is not an attempt to evangelise for any one view. Rather, it attempts to show how many people have different views, and that for the successful resolution of conflicts, we all need to be aware of those many different ways of approaching a common set of problems.

The modern world is awash with arguments about the environment. Membership of environmental groups is flourishing: both the established preservation societies such as the RSPB,[1] The National Trust, the local Naturalists Trusts; and the more campaigning organisations such as Friends of the Earth and Greenpeace. There are also political parties with an explicitly environmental agenda: the "Green Party". This movement is not restricted to the UK, indeed it could be argued it has been led from outside. There is now European legislation leading the way: the European Habitats Directive and legislation for the protection of water (the European Water Framework Directive) and air, and international treaties such as the Ramsar Convention on Wetlands. A history of the Environmental movement is given by McCormick (1995), an illuminating analysis of the progress of environmental concern in the political sphere by Dryzek *et al.* (2003), and the development of European Environmental Policy by Jackson (2002).

Underlying all this concern is an implicit though often un-stated ethical dimension, a dimension that tells us what we ought to do. Every time some one says, "we must preserve this natural feature," or "we must protect the environment", "we must prevent pollution", "we must act responsibly" and so on, they are making an ethical statement. The little word "must" implies an ethical content to the statement. It implies that according to some sort of value system, there is indication of how we ought to behave, a set of values that we should preserve, and so on, and these have implications for a specific environmental issue.

This book is an exploration of the role of ethics in the studies of the environment. It is not an attempt to propound a particular view of ethics, or necessarily to convince the sceptical of the virtues of the environmental movement. Rather it is an attempt to equip the reader with some of the critical apparatus to make their own decisions, to come to their own conclusions.

A brief personal note

The engagement with environmental ethics arose out of the professional life of the author. In 1975, he joined the Minis-

---

[1]   The Royal Society for the Protection of Birds.

try of Agriculture Fisheries and Food as a Research Scientist attached to the Field Drainage Experimental Unit. The remit of this unit was to improve the science underlying the practice of field drainage, which was then receiving grant aid at a rate up to 60% of the capital cost. This was all part of the continued support to agriculture that had been a central plank of government agricultural policy since the 1939-45 war (Martin, 2000), and which had been restated in a government white paper the same year: *Food from our own resources* (MAFF, 1975).

Subsequently, the author became a non-stipendiary priest in the Church of England, serving the church on Sundays and in the evenings, whilst remaining an active scientist during the working day. This book is in part an outcome of the creative tensions introduced by this dual role, as a scientist and as a priest, and the way the two interact: the environmental scientist posing the questions, and theological reflection positing some of the possible answers. The same material was then used as a starting point for a series of lectures on environmental ethics at the University of Birmingham Department of Geography, forming a component of an "Environmental Management" course.

There has also been significant interest from my colleagues, both academics and environmental professionals. Papers presented at conferences (Armstrong, 2000, 2006, & 2007) have generated interest, and a whole workshop (with European Science Foundation funding) was devoted to the ethics of wetland management. This essay is aimed as much at those professional colleagues as to my students.

This personal explanation also places the whole work in the context of the UK and the Christian religion. A parallel book could be written in another country from another tradition, but it would be very different, and I would be unable to write it.

What do we mean by ethics?

Ethics is the study of how we ought to behave, and how we reach decisions about our actions. It is primarily concerned with the way human beings decide what is right and what is wrong, and how they then apply those insights in their everyday behaviour. It is thus concerned with defining what is the correct thing to do in a given situation. If the characteristic word that gives any statement an ethical status is "must", then ethics is the study of the answering question: "why?" Ethics as a study area thus seeks to identify the reasons for adopting certain modes of behaviour, and for making certain decisions.

Ethics can be a deeply philosophical study, concerned with abstract relations between value systems, or it can be an immensely practical study concerned with the articulation of issues in specific circumstances. It can also be viewed as an essentially religious study, or a sociological one seeing how societies work out their decisions and how they support them. In this book, ethics are taken in the sense of practical ethics, of what is right and wrong in a specific subject area, which is the care for the environment. We thus ask how we reach ethical decisions relating to our care of the environment and the natural world.

A brief survey of the literature reveals an enormous number of approaches to ethics, both amongst the philosophers who have debated how to reach ethical decisions, and those who have proposed ethical systems. Indeed, ethics has been an essential component of all philosophy as far as it has been about human behaviour. Equally, nearly all religious systems have included ethical statements in their doctrines. So whereas the first systematic exposition of ethics is that of Aristotle, dating to the fifth century BC, the Bible contains in its first five book ethical codes going back probably a millennium before that; and even older codes can be found in the eastern religions (reflected for example in the teachings of the Buddha and Confucius). It is thus useful to identify a few of the various bases for thinking about ethics, and particularly the terminology they use. These relate specifically to the question of the sources of ethical understanding, and the definition of right and wrong that flows from them. They are thus to be distinguished from practical ethics, which addresses the issues associated with a particular application (such as environmental ethics, which is the subject of this book).

Natural ethics

By "natural ethics" we refer to that component of ethical thinking that finds the source of its inspiration in nature. Although nature itself is a very difficult concept to handle, having a whole variety of meanings, many of which are socially and culturally defined, there is a central thought that there are a series of self-evident "natural" concepts, which define the basis for ethics. We might immediately identify the respect for human life as one such "natural" concept. If we can all agree what the core of natural ethics is, then we can develop a rule for life based on this common basis. The problem is that whilst it is easy enough to talk about "natural" principles, it is less easy to identify them, and even less easy to agree about them. Nevertheless, despite the problems (which are discussed in more detail in Chapter 3, pp. 37–40), this approach does demonstrate a common thread to all ethics: that the basis for ethical behaviour can be defined in terms of some prior set of principles that are then used for deducing the correct modes of behaviour in specific circumstances.

Rational ethics

By "rational ethics" we refer to those who would find the basis for their ethics in rational thought. This is similar in many ways to the naturalist approach, except the basis is not any set of "natural" principles, but those principles that can be derived from a rational reflection on human behaviour. The immediate difficulty is that human beings have not yet managed to come up with a consensus of what constitutes right rational behaviour (I suspect they never will). Consequently, owing to the lack of universally agreed principles, it is almost impossible to derive an agreed definition of good and bad actions to underlie decisions about practical actions.

Theistic ethics

"Theistic ethics" solves the problem of the derivation of the base principles by the appeal to a religious authority. Normally, they claim a revelation of a set of principles that enables the adherents to discern the will of their god, and their expression in an ethical system. A classical example is the *Torah* of Jewish scripture, which defines the modes of behaviour for Jews and Christians alike, by defining a set of rules governing, in some detail, almost every aspect of the life of the people to whom they were originally given. There are many problems with such revelations, particularly when they become historical and fail to provide answers to current questions. The Bible, for example, does not mention climate change, or open-heart surgery, or many other of the issues facing life in the twenty-first century. It is now left to the adherents of the religions to find solutions to their current issues in the light of the original revelation. An additional problem with religions based on an historical revelation is that most of them have a sufficiently rich combination of sources and subsequent teachings that it is difficult to provide a single and unambiguous set of principles that can be immediately identified as relevant to current situations. For example, in the Christian religion (the one I know best) it is possible to identify a real and continued tension between those who insist on a literalist interpretation and application of the commandments they find in the Bible, and those who find a more liberal and less absolute situationist interpretation of ethics based on the underlying principle of Christian love.

Consequentalist ethics

Another major distinction that needs to be made at the start is the difference between consequentialist and intrinsic ethics. Consequentalist ethics can be caricatured by the slogans "the ends justify the means" and "you are responsible for your actions." Such ethical thinking examines cases almost exclusively in terms of their consequences, and so will either justify or ethically question an act in terms of the good or evil that follows from it. Serious use of this sort of approach to ethics however inevitably raises the issue of how to evaluate different consequences. In environmental terms, this can for example turn into an argument about how we value the essential non-material benefit of a healthy environment against the extremely accountable benefits of modern developments. So how do we weigh up the benefits of a bypass (which can be evaluated in terms of travel times and travel costs) against the loss of a beautiful landscape, or the habitat of a rare species of invertebrate? The strict consequentialist says this is a technical matter for economic or social evaluation, and that in principle it can and should be done, as the best way of making decisions.

Intrinsic ethics

Intrinsic ethics will have none of this, but argues that there are some things that are intrinsically right or wrong in themselves, and cannot be "negotiated" away by some argument for a good consequence. This might seem to be the province of the religious, but in fact there seems to be an underlying set of intrinsic values, such as the existence of an entire species, or the value of a human life for example, which seem almost like the absolutes that we might use as a basis for "Natural" ethics. Inevitably we then come against practical examples where apparent absolutes appear to conflict. I remember being told one story when I was at school (which I cannot now trace) about a group of children and their guide trapped in an arctic winter storm. The guide (the mother of some or all of the children) killed the weakest, which they ate, while all the others survived and were rescued. This seems repulsive to us, but the action was apparently not only accepted but also praised by the society within which the action was taken. A less extreme example is observable in the situation in which a group of armed gamekeepers meet a group of armed poachers. Should they engage the poachers, at the risk of killing one of them, or of being killed themselves? The issue could be seen in terms of enforcing laws, but it could also be seen in terms of the relative values of human and animal lives. Is the intrinsic worth of human life so great that we should not engage in a situation where a life is threatened, no matter how great the consequence?

These sorts of examples might be multiplied almost indefinitely, but they show how difficult it is to apply absolute standards without reaching logical absurdities. On the other hand, reducing every decision to its consequences can be unhelpful when it has no absolute standards to value the differences between the outcomes of a decision.

Words and their meanings

The whole of the debate about the environment is a terminological nightmare. Words are often bandied around and used in ways that hide a whole confusion of meanings. Even the basic word, "environment" has a variety of meanings, both popular and technical. Whilst it has a technical meaning of all that surrounds any object of study, the word has currently acquired a whole raft of popular meanings, to represent the whole issue of concern for the natural world, and human beings' relations with it. In particular it has come to represent the range of issues that relate to the protection of the natural world from the depredations of human activity, and so encompasses issues such the global climate, the fate of rain forests, the fate of rare animals, and the preservation of wilderness areas, what we call in a convenient shorthand the "Green movement".

This of course then raises the issue of what we mean by nature, and the related term natural. Here the main theme is that nature is the rest of the world, apart from human beings (Evernden, 1992). The natural state of the world is that before human beings grew to their current state of culture and so before they altered their environment significantly. There is also a strong thread identifying "natural" behaviour as those ways human beings are thought to have behaved in a pre-cultural state; or ways in which human beings appear to behave that reflect the behaviour of animals (see e.g. Midgley, 1978). These issues will be discussed in Chapter 3, pp. 30–33. In the light of the terminological difficulties, a few definitions are given that will be used, so far as is possible, throughout this book:

Environment, concern for. This will be used in its popular meaning of a concern for all things relating to the world beyond human beings. This embraces not only animals, but also whole ecosystems, and indeed the whole of the Earth. It is almost everywhere used as a term with ethical overtones.

Nature will also be used in its popular meaning, which is almost equal to the environment, and certainly the non-human world. It will be used generally as a term of identification, without any explicit overtones of concern or ethical value.

Men. Although I will attempt to use a genderless language, almost inevitably some of the quotes, if not my own writing, reverts to a pre-politically correct usage. It will always mean the whole of human kind, unless explicitly noted otherwise. I apologise to readers who find this usage offensive, but I cannot retrospectively re-write what has already been written.

Ecology is used popularly in much the same way as the "environment," to imply not so much the study of ecosystems as the actions to protect them from degradation, or a philosophical stance on these issues (e.g. "Deep Ecology", see p. 77). The technical sense of ecology as the study of systems in the environment is generally restricted to the biological sciences (e.g. Odum, 1966). I use it generally in this second sense, although other sources quoted may use it in the more popular sense. Consequently, to avoid confusion, this term is generally avoided wherever possible.

Sustainability is a term that is much used in environmental discourses, and has become used so widely that it can mean almost anything. Generally, it implies a care to ensure that non-renewable resources are not used profligately, but are instead harboured and used only where necessary. It is widely used in the agricultural context to imply a land management system that does not degrade soil or other resources, but rather builds up soil fertility and so safe-guards the future. The issue is discussed in more detail in Chapter 5 (see p. 64).

Chapter 2

Some origins of environmental ethics

This is not the place to write a history of ethics. It is nevertheless helpful to identify some of the significant contributions that form the historical backdrop to this study. In doing so, I will try to maintain an emphasis on the development of ideas that relate to the issue of the environment, and humanities' relationship to it, rather than a pure theory of ethics approach. (This explains some significant omissions of writers who are considered important from a purely philosophical perspective.) In the context and constraints of this essay, I can only identify a few highlights that introduce ideas that will be used later. A more comprehensive approach is given for example in the collection of essays in Jamieson (2001).

The Greek legacy

Almost inevitably, any discussion of philosophy has to start with the ancient Greeks, the amazing flowering of civilisation and thought that flowered particularly in Periclean Athens of the fifth century BC, but which embraced the whole of the Eastern Mediterranean civilisation. The earliest Greek, pre-Socratic, philosophers appeared to see the universe as one in which the world and the life in it are inseparable. They also thought that human beings should take as their example and inspiration the ordered function of the universe (particularly the stars and the Earth's seasons), and try to emulate this in their lives. Both they and Socrates come close to seeing the underlying rationality of the universe, the *logos,* in divine terms, a theme that recurs in the Christian understanding of the universe, particularly the prologue to John's gospel. The all-inclusive non-anthropocentric view of the end of the universe in a divine world certainly leads to a wider human concern for the whole universe, which might then have been developed into an environmental ethic, although this is a step the Greeks never took (Carone, 2001).

The major figures in Greek philosophy are Socrates and Aristotle. For both of them, the goal of human life was the attainment of happiness, which was to be achieved by the pursuit of virtue. This goal was described in ways that were exclusively relevant to the free (and that meant upper class) male head of a Greek household of the fifth century BC: a life that was well ordered, measured, and secure. There is no room for passion, no room for love. Russell (1945, chapter XX) is particularly scathing when, after an extensive quote from Aristotle's description of a "magnanimous man", he comments "one shudders to think what a vain man would be like".

To Aristotle, ethics was then concerned almost exclusively with social behaviour, so there was an overlap between ethics and politics. Greek ethics thus appears to consider a society ethically satisfactory where there is stability and peace and order, even though the fruits of these virtues are restricted to only a few, and the vast majority have severe restrictions on their personal lives, many living in actual slavery. The virtues of stability and order of the society thus transcend the requirement for justice for the individual. In fact, most of the Greeks would have not considered the question of rights of their slave labourers as even a valid issue for concern. In response, however repulsive we find the Greek attitudes to slaves, we must be careful not to attack an historical culture with the presuppositions of our own understanding. Nevertheless, to Aristotelian ethics, the highest virtue is for the few, whose aim is to attain the greatest good for the community, not for the individual.

There is thus little in Greek (or at least Aristotelian) philosophy that appears to relate directly to the environment. It would be possible to extend the remit of the society that is the subject of moral consideration, to include the whole of the ecosystem, and so argue that the virtues of order and stability could well be applied to the whole Earth. However, it is less clear who would be the new lords of this order — certainly, the emphasis on the male householder would not be acceptable to women; nor would the suggestion that slavery of the many that the few can enjoy the benefits of the stability and peace be acceptable in today's more egalitarian society. It would, however, be unwise to dismiss Aristotle quite so cavalierly, if for no other reason than it has been a major source of philosophical thinking about ethics ever since (see e.g. Weldon, 1987; Barnes, 1995; Sherman, 1999), and has indeed been used for the development of an environmental ethic by Foster (2002).

Aristotle's views on the natural world are additionally to be found in his descriptions of that world, in which he took a relatively modern (and then revolutionary) scientific view of the universe, which has formed the basis of much scientific discussion since. Aristotle saw a hierarchy of beings, in which the possession of a soul applies only to higher things, and rationality only to the highest level. Such a "scale of nature", which has had a long influence on most subsequent thought, can become highly anthropocentric. This is perhaps best seen in its development in the mediaeval thought world of Aquinas.

Concentrating on the virtue theory of ethics, Foster (2002) was able to derive an environmental ethic from Aristotle. Foster first identifies the Aristotelian prerequisite that for human beings, being morally good is in their interest. Moral goodness is achieved by virtuous behaviour. Moral people therefore consider the non-human world in the same way they do the human world, because it is in the interest of all things to fulfil their nature, and so to exist in the fullest possible way. There is in addition a hierarchy of activities in living beings: from vegetable, through animal, to the uniquely human rational thought, that allows the evaluation of the importance of the various components of a moral discussion. In her exposition, Foster therefore uses the value theory underlying Aristotelian ethics as the basis for her environmentalism, rather than finding environmental attitudes themselves directly in the Greek works.

Ethical discussion can also be found in the classic literature outside the philosophical works. In particular, we may follow the lead of Nussbaum (1986) who shows that much of the Greek discussion of moral matters is to be found in its literature. In relation to the environment, we can then identify two themes.

The first is the myth of a Golden Age. The earliest expression of this is found in Hesiod's *Works and Days*. All subsequent mentions of this theme stem, directly or indirectly, from this source (West, 1998) or from the same mythological strata that Hesiod presented. Subsequent presentations of the same material are found for example in the *Metamorphoses* (Book 1) of Ovid (see Innes, 1995, for a prose translation, or Hughes, 1997, for an imaginative poetical recreation of the same Latin text). The underlying theme of this myth is that the world was previously better than it is now. In the initial Golden Age, humans (or perhaps gods) lived an idyllic life without strife and without work. Probably this myth is continuous with the Biblical myth of the Garden of Eden. What they both seem to address is the feeling that the current state of the world is not as it should be, and that it has declined from an idyllic state to its current state of hard work, warfare, and of conflict between men and beasts. Hesiod attributes this fall from the Golden Age to the actions of the gods; the Bible to the deliberate disobedience of Adam and Eve. Perhaps there is a certain amount of wishful thinking, perhaps there is the nostalgia of the city dweller for a rustic simplicity that was lost even by the eighth century BC. Nevertheless, the mythical ideal of a peaceful relation between humankind and nature, between the human race and its environment, remains a powerful vision of how the Earth might be. In that respect it offers one thread of environmental concern that is still with us: the ideal of a peaceful and plentiful Earth, a rural idyll that has remained an imagined goal for men and women over the centuries.

A second, more practical, assessment of the rural idyll is found in the classical literature, in the *Oeconomicus* of Xenophon (also called "The Estate Manager," Tredeennick & Waterfield, 1990). Here, in a discourse attributed to Socrates, a view of the life in the country is presented, in which the rural life is seen as presenting the ideal for the development of military, civic, and moral virtue. Hard work and constant preparedness is seen as the steps towards an ordered existence. A realistic view of the manager of an agricultural estate is presented as an example of the virtues of self-discipline and self-control. Here we have one of the sources of the theme that becomes common through many western attitudes to the land and the environment—the tamed, tidied nature, in which natural wildness is replaced by ordered usefulness.

The Judaeo-Christian legacy

The Judaeo-Christian tradition is probably the most influential in the Western world today, and underlies the technological domination of the world by the western European/ American civilisation, which grew out of Mediaeval Christendom. Although many other world religions have a strong sense of environmental worth, this book concentrates on the Christian tradition, for the simple reason that is the only one on which the author can speak with any authority. Readers are referred to the World Religions and Ecology series sponsored by The World Wide Fund for Nature, for discussions of Hinduism by Prime (1992), Islam by Khalid & O'Brien (1992), Buddhism by Batchelor & Brown (1992), Judaism by Rose (1992), as well as the parallel text on Christianity by Breuilly & Palmer (1992). These traditions are also reviewed in Jamieson (2001), Singer (1991), Tucker & Williams, (1997) and in the essays edited by Priscoli *et al.* (2004).

There is within the Christian tradition a strong and very real concern for the land, initially coming from the Jewish experience of life on the edge of a desert, which saw the reign of God in terms of the Promised Land, a land "flowing with milk and honey". However, the same tradition also contains within it an ascetic streak that would deny the world in order to concentrate on spiritual matters. From an emphasis on inner holiness, in which the need to attain salvation is paramount, it is possible to find discussions which consider the Earth not as our home where we belong, but as hotel, through which we pass, merely a staging post on our way to heaven (e.g. Murphy, 1989).

Further traditions within Christianity have also been seen as inimical to the environment, in particular the injunction to subdue the Earth, taken from Genesis 1.28, which has been seen as the licence to exploit and to control the Earth, an attitude that has been claimed to lie at the centre of the current environmental problems (White, 1967). This exploitative attitude was further developed into the Calvinist work ethic, which saw idle land as an offence against God, and so sought to bring it to the useful and therefore godly condition of cultivation.

The accusation of being either too otherworldly, or too exploitative has in general given Christianity a "bad press" in environmental circles. Nevertheless, there is a real sense in which Christianity has at its core the central insight that "The Earth is the Lord's" (Psalm 24.1) and so puts humanity in a position of being responsible to God for what it does with the creation. This provides one basis for the concept of Stewardship that has been popular in recent years, and underlines the thinking behind many modern discussions of sustainability.

Mediaeval thought

The period up to the Renaissance was rich and varied in thought, but it is possible to identify a few main streams, in quite generalised terms. In the main, all philosophy, all ethics, indeed all education, was the province of the church, and theology was the "Queen of the Sciences". In an age when life expectancies were low, infant mortality rates high, plague and pestilence rife, and warfare frequent, it was perhaps inevitable that philosophy and theology should concentrate on achieving salvation in the next world. It was in this context that the mediaeval church could concentrate its efforts on earning a way to heaven, when life here on Earth was so uncertain. The prime theologian of the middle ages, St Thomas Aquinas, was thus concerned to offer a synthesis of Aristotelian thought and salvation-oriented theology. Life on Earth was seen as the "vale of soul-making", as a preparation for heaven. The Earth was thus provided solely for use by humankind on its journey to heaven, and so was not morally considerable. Hence, Aquinas could say that cruelty to animals (characterised as "brute beasts") was morally neutral unless it led to habits of cruelty and sin (Linzey, 1994). A similar argument has also been identified in the much later writing of Kant by Midgley, (1983), who rejected it as "frivolous".[1]

Equally strong, in at least the mediaeval popular imagination, was the horror of failing to achieve salvation, and being cast into the everlasting punishment of hell. This world-view may seem crude to us, but it found beautiful expression in the poetry of Dante, and in the developing religious art, particularly in Italy.

Of course, there were other strands of thought. Particularly relevant is that of St Francis of Assisi. A truly remarkable man, he rejected his life as a member of the rich and privileged classes, and adopted a life of poverty devoted to God. What was particularly remarkable was that his vision of the circle of salvation included the whole of the world. There are stories that he preached to the birds, and taught wolves the error of their ravenous ways.[2] He could refer to

---

[1]   Midgley actually states: "Anyone who refrained from cruelty *merely* from a wish not to sully his own character, without any direct consideration for the possible victims, would be frivolous and narcissistic" (Author's italics). Page 95 of the 1995 reprint.

[2]   It does not matter whether Francis actually performed these acts. The fact that he was thought to have done so, and that these (possibly apocryphal) acts were widely reported and used for teaching, gave these attitudes the authority of the Saint, that has rendered them influential ever since.

the Earth and sun, wind and water and the moon as brother and sister.[3] It is clear he considered the created order as worthy of moral consideration, and indeed to be loved. For this reason, White (1967) offered Francis as the patron saint of ecological Christianity. For the current purpose, Francis is probably most important in that he acts as a figurehead for a whole strand of mediaeval theology, which would seek to affirm and enjoy life on this Earth. He therefore demonstrated that the mediaeval thought world was much richer than the simple exposition of Thomist orthodoxy.

Rationalism

The Renaissance of the fifteenth century opened the intellectual world beyond the confines of theology. The concepts of Nature and Natural had been perhaps redefined, certainly more sharply defined, at the Renaissance (Evernden, 1992). The discovery of the New World and the Far East in the sixteenth century opened up the geographical limits and horizons of thought, and the burgeoning "Natural Philosophy", what we now call science, of the seventeenth century opened up both a new intellectual territory for exploration, and a new source of truth, that of experimental evidence. One crucial step was the adoption of the heliocentric model of the universe and the corresponding adoption of a less anthropocentric view. All these elements, combined with many more, gave the impetus to the growth of a rational re-thinking of the bases of philosophy, which flowered in the eighteenth century that is normally given the name: The "Enlightenment".

This great flowering of human rationalism took a completely new look at the way human beings saw themselves in relation to the Earth and the heavens. It was perhaps an age of confidence, in which the rationalism of human beings was taken as a new standard (Taliaferro, 2003). This gave a new ground for the age-old separation of humankind from

[3] Francis' Canticle of the Sun has been anglicised into the well-known hymn "All creatures of our God and King". The original is available in many sources, among them Everitt *et al.* (1985).

the natural world, that of the possession of a rational mind (so replacing the mediaeval assessment that gave human beings a special role because they alone possessed an immortal soul). In this optimistic assessment, the role of humankind as the measure of the Earth was again affirmed. In this sort of intellectual environment, the Calvinistic work ethic could easily be applied to the Earth — so that land that was not useful, but idle, was considered an offence against the ethical standards of hard work and usefulness.

The Darwinian revolution

The next great revision in the way we thought about ourselves was the consequence of the publication in 1859 of Darwin's *The origin of species*. The reaction to this book was one of the mainsprings of scientific and theological thought for much of the second half of the nineteenth century. This has been widely documented and discussed by many authors, particularly those concerned to put the record straight after the supposed rift between science and religions (e.g. Brooke & Cantor, 1998). The major impact of the Darwinian synthesis was to return humankind to its true place as part of the natural world. *Homo sapiens*, evolved from a sequence of primates and great apes, is in biological terms just another species on the Earth. Modern biology has expanded the depth of our understanding of this statement by observing that 95% of our DNA is the same as that of the chimpanzees. It has thus become impossible to see the human race as apart from or superior to the other inhabitants of the Earth. We are in a sense, just a particularly successful species, rushing to a catastrophe caused by a population explosion. In terms of environmental ethics, it is thus no longer possible to separate ourselves from the world around us. Whilst we may argue that we have no contractual obligations to the animals, we cannot deny that we share much of their basic biology. (This is discussed in more detail in the following chapter.)

Modern scientism

In the twentieth century, a gradual arrogance in the scientific world view, in parallel with the growing success of the scientific enterprise, has led to a new reliance on science that some (who regard the development as malign) label as the new religion of scientism. Science, it seems, can do anything, explain everything: it can see the fundamental particles of matter, and describe the origins of the universe back to the Big Bang. It has thus replaced religion as a means of explaining anything and everything, and with that change, the human race has "grown up" and so abandoned a childish reliance on religion. Some parts of the scientific enterprise even see religion as the result of a defective or aberrant gene (e.g. Dawkins, 1976). Scientism is perhaps not so much a serious philosophical theory, but it is certainly a component of the popular reliance on science and technology to solve all problems, including those associated with the environment, while specifically rejecting religion.[4] If technology fails, the answer is more and better technology. If science cannot understand something, it just needs more research. Such a reliance on science and technology would, unchecked, become a totally anthropocentric worldview. The environment would be reduced to a source of resources, or a source of pleasures to be managed.

Ecofeminism

A very strong modern tradition, based on a feminist approach, argues that many of the current ills of the environment arise from the essentially masculine domination of western society; and that an alternative feminist approach has much to offer the environment. This view, termed "Ecofeminism", covers a very wide spectrum of views, and includes both mainstream views and some less so. (One author, Keller, 1994, tells us that "Talk about the weather therefore becomes ecofeminist discourse", so just remem-

---

[4]   It is of course both proper and sensible to separate science from technology, but in the populist view of scientism this differentiation is seldom made.

ber that next time you watch the forecast!) Radford Ruether (1992, pp. 1–2), identifies some of the important themes and subdivisions of both ecology and feminism.

The central concept behind the ecofeminist movement is that there are two basic things wrong with the world at present: the domination of women by men, and the domination of nature by humankind. By identifying the two as aspects of the same basic phenomenon, male dominance, ecofeminists thus join the forces of feminism and ecological concern, to offer an alternative view of the way we interact with creation.

> Ecofeminism explores how male domination of women and domination of nature are interconnected, both in cultural ideology and in social structures (Radford Ruether, 1992, p. 2).

The link between these two attitudes is, it is claimed, to be found in the origins of scientific thinking. The language of the seventeenth and eighteenth centuries' science appears to speak of the subjugation of a female Nature by a rational male man. The exploitation of Nature by men can then be seen as one and the same phenomenon as the exploitation of women by men, particularly among those who see many of the evils of the current age as due to the scientific "domination" of the natural world. In doing so they frequently quote the works of Francis Bacon, who described the scientific method in terms which are full of references to the domination, the subjection, the rape even, of a feminine nature by rational scientific men.

> For Bacon, scientific knowledge is fundamentally a tool of power, the capacity to subjugate and rule over "nature" (Radford Ruether, 1992, p. 195).

In addition, because Nature is identified with Eve, the scientific domination of man over Nature is one with the social domination of men over women.

In response, it is probably incontrovertible that society has, for perhaps more than three thousand years, been fundamentally patriarchal in its organisation and attitudes, and is still so in many respects. Western society as a whole is still working out the implication of that change of attitudes that we call the Emancipation of Women. It is equally incontrovertible that society as a whole has a dominating attitude towards the natural world. Nature is a source of resources ("Natural Resources") to be tapped and tamed; the needs of the human animal take precedent over all other species, even to the extent of extinction; unused land is seen as ripe for "reclamation" for agriculture. The issue that needs to be decided is whether these are facets of the same basic problem, related but separate problems, or merely two unrelated issues in parallel. I suspect that the case is by no means as obviously clear as the ecofeminist would have us believe.

The ecofeminist argument is further not without its difficulties. It looks very much as though the feminists have identified one good source text in the writings of Bacon, and repeatedly re-quoted it without asking the question of whether the source is either typical or much regarded. (This point is made by Clark, 1993). Most scientists do not read Bacon. Many (possibly most) do not read either the philosophy or the history of their particular branch of science at all. The language of domination and exploitation is absent in standard accounts of the philosophy of science (e.g. Carnap, 1966; Popper, 1935; Toulmin, 1953), and the scientific method is more normally seen today as a search after truth, or an investigation into, and an exploration of, a rich and diverse universe. Domination and control may be the aims of much technology that is science based, but it is difficult to identify control with the aims of modern science as they are commonly reported. It is, on the other hand, equally possible that the ideas of domination have just become so much part of our subconscious culture that we are not even aware of them.

It is also perhaps inevitable that any discussion of the role of the female in society eventually comes to the issue of fertility. The role of the feminine in the creation of new life is a continuous source of mystery and amazement to humankind, even in these days of clinical gynaecology. Every society has, it seems, an inherent awe of that mystery. Ultimately, the continuation of humanity rests on it, and that is why control of it is so important. Perhaps we are seeing here a vestige of the pre-conscious biological differentiation of roles. It is because of its importance, that the differentiation between male and female is so basic both to our understanding of ourselves as beings, and to all societies, that it further appears as a dominant theme in the social expression of many religions.

Consequently, for much of the Christian era, Nature has been seen as something wild and untamed, a source both of fecundity and of evil, which has then been identified with Eve, the archetypal woman and temptress. The rationality of man has been seen as the answer to the fallen-ness of woman. Feminists want, not unreasonably, to reject much of that picture. Even though it is useful to retain the insight that the natural state is in some way a jungle of unfettered emotion and sexual symbol, it is necessary to reject the simplistic notion both that the root of all the problems lies with femininity, and that it needs to be controlled by rational masculinity. It seems better to argue that the dark side of humanity, which can be identified with the irrational and the "natural", is common to both sexes.

Hierarchical and holistic modes of thought

Some feminists identify the modern scientific thought pattern as hierarchical and dominating, and thus part of the mechanism for the subjugation of both women and nature. They argue that there is an alternative, distinctively feminine, way of thought, which is Holistic as opposed to Hierarchical, all-embracing as opposed to Dualist.

Nevertheless, both hierarchies and dualisms are very useful tools, as exemplified by the Aristotelian great chain of being. The whole Linnaean system for classifying living things into kingdoms, genera, phyla, species, is a wonderful way of organising the information, and the very act of imparting organisation gives us information as well: species close to each other in the hierarchical tree are likely to behave similarly in some respects.

By contrast, the holistic approach wants to empathise with all there is in any situation. Faced with an ecological problem it would empathetically absorb the information about all there is, but in practice, when faced with any real problem, such an approach just goes into information overload. The human brain cannot handle the amount of information that a totally holistic understanding of any situation would require. Nevertheless, for many ecological problems, a holistic viewpoint is an advantage, an antidote to the situations where a problem is split between many experts each of whom examine a small component of a problem, with no one to take an overview, although this is not to deny the value of analytical thought.

In response, it can be argued that one of the great advances we have made in our social thinking over the last hundred or so years, is the acceptance of the view that men and women are equal in moral, personal, social and political terms. We have a society in which the sexes are at least theoretically equal. Consequently, we need to take away gender attribution of attitudes. So I would argue, we need to identify dominant and passive roles, not male and female roles; good and bad thought, not male and female thought patterns. In this, the great achievement of the ecofeminists has been the identification of both the problem and its solution in the development of new and more harmonious interactions between humans and the Earth (Smith, 1997). This normally also involves a retrieval of the sense of the sacred in the Earth, and is thus often seen as recapturing the insights of the pre-Christian religions, notably those of the native Americans and similar cultures. In response, Third World ecofeminist perspective itself often offers a critique of First World ecofeminism, which it can easily identify as a pastime for the affluent (Radford Ruether, 1996; Smith, 1997).

Ecofeminism thus offers an alternative vision for the Earth, in which relationships are more important than domination and control. Ecofeminists are thus less concerned about the rights of the subject (animals, plants, even rocks), than on the need into enter into a relationship with all of them, within a vision of a mutual and reciprocal interdependence.

The rise of modern environmentalism

The last phase in the development of environmental ethics is the emergence of a modern environmentalism. The rise of the environmental movement over the last 100 years has been chronicled by McCormick (1995), and a political commentary offered by Dryzek *et al.* (2003). Although the roots of American environmentalism can be traced to the middle of the nineteenth century, in works such as Thoreau's *Walden* (1854), Marsh's *Man and Nature* (Lowenthal, 1965), and the pioneering actions of men such as John Muir (Cronon, 1997; Turner, 1997), many of the issues that were raised at that time were not really debated and received little professional philosophical discussion. Rather, the initial impetus was for the preservation of wilderness areas, which then further developed into the establishment of preservation bodies, in what was an essentially practical movement, not a philosophical one. The same could be said of the re-launch of the environmental movement in the 1960s with the publication of Rachel Carson's *Silent Spring* (1962) which was a *crie de coeur* about a perceived wrong. Perhaps the shining example of an alternative approach to thinking about the environment is the justly famous *Sand County Almanac* of Aldo Leopold (1949), which proposed a "Land Ethic", that has become the basis of much recent discussion. Leopold's land ethic first extends the boundary of the community in which we function to include "soils, water, plants, and animals, or collectively: the land," so turning human beings from conquerors to plain citizens of the land community. The land ethic is stated simply: "A thing is right when it tends to preserve the integrity, stability and beauty of the biotic community. It is wrong when it tends otherwise."

There are, additionally, many strands to modern environmental philosophy, including the Deep Ecology movement, ecofeminism, environmental economics, and animal rights, some of which will be described and discussed in chapter 5 of this book.

Despite its concentration on the practical issues, the environmental movement has been supported by a philosophical discussion, in the attempt to identify the underpinning rationale for the movement. Subsequently, Elliot (1995) noted that the consideration of the non-human component by environmentalist philosophers was both challenging and novel. To him, extending the sphere of moral thinking to include the non-human world as objects of moral consideration was a significant step forward in philosophy. Although the recent environmental movement has been led by its concern for practical issues, it has been followed by a subsequent philosophical exploration of the issues it has raised. The environmental movement has thus been firmly rooted in the *praxis* (the doing) of preserving the environment, and philosophical considerations have followed.

Chapter 3

Humanity and naturalness

This chapter considers the fundamental question about ourselves as human beings: how do we relate to things around us? Much of the way we relate to our environment comes out of that understanding. It is after all one of the fundamental issues of philosophy, put (in non-PC terms) in the old question: what is man? Again, as in the rest of this book, our immediate concern is not to identify a single way of answering this question, but to identify the numerous strands that have developed, all of which are competing (or rather, complementary) ways of looking at ourselves. We are accustomed to the use of phrases such as: we are political animals; we are social animals; we are sexual animals; we are economic animals: we are just animals. The multiplicity of insights, all partly true, offered by such aphorisms identifies part of our multi-facetted human nature. Against this, we need to consider how we identify ourselves over and against our environment: how we learn to classify and categorise our surroundings, and therefore how we view, use and relate to them. This chapter thus identifies a number of ways of looking at our surroundings and ourselves. In particular, it considers first the anthropological perspective on humanity, and then discusses the terms Nature and Naturalness.

The answers can perhaps be split into two major groups — those that would identify humankind as something separate from and distinct from the natural world, and those that would emphasise the continuity of humankind with the rest of the natural world. We have already noted in the previous chapter that the Darwinian narrative of the evolution of homo sapiens had removed the grounds for special pleading in favour of a special creation of the human race.[1]

The anthropological perspective

According to the geological and anthropological evidence, the human race evolved from the early hominids, probably in Africa, and from there spread to cover the whole of the Earth.[2] Although this is a subject where much research remains to be done, and for which the fossil evidence is still emerging, the main lines of human evolution seem to be well defined, and the origins of the human species in Eastern Africa is both clear and generally agreed. It seems that several species of primates existed in Africa, and some of them evolved into early human-like species during the early Pleistocene (over the past 2,000,000 years), apparently under the evolutionary pressure of the rapidly changing climates of the glacial epochs. From the African origins, early hominids dispersed around the globe, particularly in the tropical regions. Despite counter-claims, it seems that most anthropologists accept an African origin, and the early hominids found for example in the Far East (Peking and Java man) are examples of species that have spread out from Africa. Anthropologists trace the evolution of human characteristics (the erect walk, the gripping hand, the increasing intelligence signified by the greater skull size) along with an increasingly wide diet and most significantly the gradual development of early tools.

The geological perspective shows us that human beings are a very new arrival on the planet. The Earth is approximately 4,000 million years old. Life appeared perhaps 2,000

[1]   To be quite clear, I accept the current scientific Darwinian synthesis, and do not find it in any way contrary to my religious beliefs. The first three chapters of Genesis are a marvellous and resonant poetical reflection on the wonders of creation and our dependence on a creator God, but they are most emphatically NOT an authoritative narrative of the creation of the world.

[2]   My source of information is Bonting (2005, pp. 37–41): a summary of data repeated in many texts.

million years ago, the first fossils date from about 1,600 million years ago. Human beings are thus so far a very short-lived species. If nothing else, we need to view the vastness of geological time from a position of humility. From the geological perspective, we could equally consider the human race as nothing more than a particularly effective primate. We can see ourselves as part of, and place ourselves within, the great evolutionary stream that stretches back to the earliest origins of life in the remote geological past. From this perspective, we human beings are in many ways similar to much of the natural world. The architecture of our bodies, the nature and arrangement of our internal organs, the nature of our biochemistry, shows continuity with the whole of the animal kingdom, and we share much of our DNA with the other great apes. In these terms, we are not exceptional.

We are part of the natural ecosystem, and we also have to accept that if the human species were to became extinct it would affect the survival of only a minute fraction of other organisms: those few parasites that have become specific to ourselves. We have only a small unique part in the functioning of natural ecosystems: although equally our activities are essential to the continued functioning of many seminatural or wholly anthropogenic systems.

Humanity as part of the natural world

A modern scientific understanding of humanity would therefore reject the separation of humankind from the rest of the natural order, stressing the observation that human beings are continuous with the rest of the natural order, sharing their genes with it, and having evolved from it. It is no longer possible to claim (as the mediaeval theologians did) that humankind is a separate order of being, created separate and superior to the rest of the natural world. Consequently, many thinkers now seek to understand the place of the human race in the natural order. It is perhaps the underlying insight of the Deep Ecology movement that it takes as its starting point the integration of human nature within a natural system.

It can thus be argued that human beings are just particularly successful animals. Many species alter their environment extensively (termites build mounds, birds build nests, beavers build damns, chimpanzees and gorillas build shelters). Several colonial insects, among them termites and bees, create controlled environments, in which they follow a life of strict division and industry. From one perspective, humanity is just doing the same thing, although in a bigger (possibly better) way. Consequently, when we observe human beings building artificial ecosystems, we could suggest that they are using their "natural" nest-building skills in a way that surpasses other species only in its effectiveness and extensiveness. Equally, species continue to compete one with another and the weaker is destroyed, or marginalised, a process we can observe repeated in the geological record, and as we ourselves displaced our Neanderthal contemporaries.

So, it can be argued, human beings do only what many species do, the difference being that they do it more efficiently and on a bigger scale. To which the counter-argument is that human beings alone have the captivity for reflecting on what they are doing, and evaluating their actions. They thus have the moral and ethical capacity to consider what they have done, which gives them a unique position and responsibility.

Natural behaviour

This discussion of human beings as part of the natural world leads to a consideration of the meanings of the words Nature and Naturalness. These words are used both colloquially and technically, often uncritically, and with varying degrees of precision. At an early age, we learn of "Nature" as short hand for the non-human world, in particular in its undisturbed state. A standard item of the early school years is a "Nature table." Nature thus contains flowers, animals, sometimes insects, sometimes rocks and stones. It is the non-human world: an object for curiosity and to be investigated, perhaps valued and preserved, but certainly separate and different from human beings. Infants are taught this at an early age. Gradually we come to distinguish the categories of things, and then to aggregate them into "natural" and man-made. Whereas the distinction between human and non-human can perhaps be considered to be simple biology, the lumping together of a whole category of objects into "Nature" is a learnt concept. Like all learnt concepts it embodies many of the ways societies see themselves, and is in some ways is best seen as a social issue. This is, in summary, the argument of Evernden (1992). Before we examine that notion, we must also note that the term "natural" has other equally powerful meanings, notably those that describe what it is in a being's "nature" to do. So there is a residual element of what is "natural" in the activities of all human beings; and the popular usage often excuses actions: its only natural. This then raises the issue of "natural behaviour."[3]

A recent spate of books has done much to popularise the ideas that humankind still retains many behavioural traits that appear to be continuous with the natural world, derived in part from the writings of Konrad Lorenz (discussed for example in Stevenson, 1974). In them, aspects of human behaviour that appear to be derived from our animal natures: aggression, territoriality, feeding, and sexuality are identified. (The whole issue is reviewed pithily by Midgley, 1979.) Some aspects of animal behaviour can appear to be biologically controlled, and are generally described as "instinctive". Quite complex behaviours of many animals (such as migration, mating rituals and nest building) are explained in this way, and it is argued that some aspects of human behaviour must be similarly conditioned: "hard-wired" as it were. On this basis it is easy to observe that human beings do indeed appear to act territorially, in a way that is common with many animal species.

---

[3] Hence the Shakespearean use of the term "Natural" to describe illegitimate children. The whole idea of Nature and Natural modes of behaviour are important themes in several of Shakespeare's plays, notably *King Lear* and *The Tempest*.

They mate and protect their mates in a way that is observed in the natural world, and so on. The examples go on, and the popularity of books describing such behaviour reflects one of the facets of the modern fascination with the "natural". In them, popular science finds in nature not only a source of wonder, but also a reflection of our own behaviours, seeking as it were an explanation (or is it an excuse) for human behaviour. The development of these traits is also seen as the product of evolution, in which the adoption of some modes of behaviour has been seen as beneficial to the survival of the species, or at least to the preservation of those modes of behaviour if they lead for example to successful mating or the successful rearing of offspring. This is the basis for Richard Dawkin's (1976) idea of the "selfish gene".

These ideas can perhaps explain some of the ways we react to our environment. The urge to reproduce, with its requirement of a safe warm environment for the rearing of children, is perhaps one source of both the urge for the built environment and for much of our social behaviour. Equally, the need to feed ourselves is the basis for our agricultural activity, and the need for land within which to hunt or in which to grow the crops is possibly a basis for human territoriality. The same biological pressures can also lead to the elimination of other competing species that would seek to use the same resources (a behaviour that is observed in some species). More problematical is the urge to violence: Lorenz sees this as a beneficial way in which the strongest males achieve mating success, in which the eldest (and hence possibly the wisest) adopt position of leadership in social animal groups.

Whilst it is clear that the human species retains some animal origins, it is also clear that much of its behaviour is learnt and socialised. Hence, "animal" has become a term of abuse. When Lorenz argues from animal behaviour (often from quite varied species), there is often a doubt whether the same drives can automatically be transferred to humankind. Nevertheless, there is a considerable popular feeling that there is such a level of explanation. Even if unproven scientifically, such an explanation is part of modern self-consciousness. It is probably better for us than the previous reflections that emphasised the separation and differences between humanity and the animal kingdom.

Perhaps we are now in a better position to understand the apparent paradox of our natures, in that we can identify the "natural" with the information content of our genes. It seems that our genes contain not only the enormous amount of information about the make up and function of our bodies, but also some behavioural traits. It is also clear that much of what makes us human is learnt. Human beings, as essentially social animals, must learn to survive as members of social units from the very start. This part of our nature is enforced by the helplessness of human babies and infants. By the time any human being is sufficiently developed, to be independent it is also inevitably and irrevocably socialised. It is thus essential that we realise that we are "much more" than animals, in that our behaviour is a complex mix containing much more than just sheer animal instincts, and we are left with the old dualism of "Nature and Nurture". Human beings are both animal and social, and the two cannot be sensibly disentangled, either in a given society or in a given human being.

From this, philosophers have developed the concept that certain things are "in our nature". These are thus the basis for a system of ethics based on our "natural behaviour". The picture has become clouded because the same word, "natural" has been used to develop the theory of "natural ethics". In particular, the discussion of the "rights of man" derives from a discussion of what is natural. Unfortunately, this cannot easily be sustained: by nature, we have no right even to exist, and have only the animal instincts to fight for survival.

Humankind as superior to the natural world

By contrast, it also seems futile to deny the one fact that we, the human race, are in some respects different from the rest of the natural world. We are different because we identify ourselves to be so. That difference is part of our consciousness. We are different because as far as we know we are the only self-aware and self-conscious animals; and we are the only species to have developed rationality as the basis for planning and executing a life style. We remember that it was the possession of rational facilities that the theologians used as the definition of human beings.

Nature is the entire non-human world. As human beings learn to distinguish themselves from it, they build a distinction between themselves and their environment. Philosophers more than most have emphasised the distinction, because the human race alone is rational, capable of analytical thought. (To which traditional religious thinkers might add that humanity alone has a soul.) In doing so, they emphasise one capacity of the human race and so elevate them to a position of importance in which they occupy a separate category of being, somewhat "higher" than the rest of the animal kingdom. One of the classic statements of this that has influenced most of Western philosophy, is to be found in the Biblical book of Psalms:

> O Lord, our Sovereign, how majestic is your name in all the Earth! You have set your glory above the heavens.
>
> Out of the mouths of babes and infants you have founded a bulwark because of your foes, to silence the enemy and the avenger.
>
> When I look at your heavens, the work of your fingers, the moon and the stars that you have established;
>
> what are human beings that you are mindful of them, mortals that you care for them?
>
> Yet you have made them a little lower than God, and crowned them with glory and honour.
>
> You have given them dominion over the works of your hands; you have put all things under their feet,
>
> all sheep and oxen, and also the beasts of the field,
>
> the birds of the air, and the fish of the sea, whatever passes along the paths of the seas.
>
> O Lord, our Sovereign, how majestic is your name in all the Earth!

Psalm 8 (New Revised Standard Version)

The hierarchical picture of the Psalm has been part of our mental furniture for most of history, with God at the top, humankind beneath, and then the rest of the created order beneath. It made a lot of sense in a hierarchical society, and if it still makes quite a lot of sense today this may well be because it is so embedded in our culture.

If we accept this hierarchical picture, we need then to consider how human kind differs, and what is the consequence of that difference. The traditional Thomist[4] theological line is that humankind alone posses a soul, and so alone can respond to its creator God. The rest of creation is then relegated merely to a subsidiary position, whose function is to provide a means of and context for the working out of our salvation. Creation is thus for the use of humankind, and has no other purpose or status. In the absolute form, this is a position of no responsibility whatsoever for the environment.[5] Cruelty to animals is then a matter of moral indifference, although not to be encouraged because it leads to the habit of cruelty; and love of animals is to be encouraged solely because it leads to the habit of loving (Linzey, 1994, pp. 12–14). Animals (and hence by implications any other component of creation) have moral status only as items of property. It is therefore immoral to kill my neighbour's ox, not because it is a cruel act, but because the victim belongs to someone else.

Against this background the concept of responsibility for the Earth has developed. On a mystical basis, there has been the development of the concept of humankind as the high priest of creation, being alone capable of responding to the creator, and so responsible to offer back to the creator the praise and thanksgiving that all creation should give. More widely influential, however, has been the tradition of stewardship and responsibility. In religious terms, humankind is seen as having a responsibility to its creator for the use it has made of the creation. Fortunately this concept has also

---

[4] Deriving from Thomas Aquinas.
[5] Though, as we have noted, this viewpoint does not exhaust the Christian response, and many, following the Franciscan line, disagree with such a negative evaluation of the world.

developed in parallel with the idea of a responsibility to all human beings, and so to all future beings, so that the crucial action now is to hand on creation undiminished to our grandchildren. From this notion developed the ideas of sustainability, so that we use the Earth in such a way as not to diminish its resources.

The notion of stewardship has been roundly rejected by Palmer (1992) as being irredeemably anthropocentric, implying a position of power and authority that the rest of the world does not acknowledge, and which some of humanity has just taken to itself. Stewardship, according to Palmer, is also a concept that relates to old modes of thought. It is a concept (or at least a word) that has been adopted because it is already to hand, whereas what we need is to replace it with a much more even-handed approach that does not assume a position of dominance by humanity. The additional criticism is that stewardship implies an essentially feudal view of the relationship; but it is not clear on whose behalf humankind is responsible for the Earth. If to God, then it implies a model of God as an absentee landlord, a view that is no longer acceptable to theology; if to the Earth itself ("Gaia"), it is not clear how the relationship is to be negotiated; or if to future generations, this again poses an awkward relationship (see below pp. 60–64). Further, the notions of stewardship are inextricably linked to the ideas of money management, as if the Earth were a resource to be managed for maximum benefit of either the occupying tenant or the absentee landlord. Palmer (p. 73) identifies a crucial statement by Pope John Paul II:

> The stewardship over nature, entrusted by God to man, will not be guided by short sightedness or selfish pursuits; rather it will take into account the fact that all created goods are directed to the good of all humanity.

Stewardship on these terms can imply a total subjugation of the natural world to the needs of humanity, and nowhere acknowledges the integrity of creation in its own right. A true environmental philosophy needs to embrace the independent rights and integrity of the natural world.

Natural law

It is commonly argued that there is a series of ethical principles that are universally acknowledged by all human beings, and which, arising from our human nature, are known as Natural Laws. The idea of natural laws goes back to the Greeks, who observed that human laws were often imperfect, and so speculated that there were "natural laws" that were the perfect underlying laws that all human laws reflected. This was in many ways parallel to the Platonic concept of ideal objects. The concept of natural law was further developed into the idea of laws that all men would recognise, as part of their nature. An example is given in St Paul's letter to the Romans (Chapter 1. 18–21) in which he claims that the divine revelation of "natural law" should be plain to all, whether Gentile or Jew.

Since then, the concept of natural law has been subject to the same sort of development as has been experienced by the concept of rights (to be discussed in Chapter 5, pp. 67–69), as thinkers have identified natural law and natural justice as self-evident processes that can be invoked at any time. Hence it is generally considered a matter of natural justice that no person may incriminate themselves, that they should be informed of the nature of any accusation against them, that they should have the right to be represented at a hearing, that they have the right to hear and interrogate their accusers, and so on. The problem with all these concepts is that is quite easy to posit the existence of natural laws, but almost impossible to identify them, and to frame them in ways that are acceptable to everybody. (A theologian might say that this is just the reflection of the imperfection of human beings: the pragmatist would be more likely to give up!)

Nevertheless, there is a general agreement that there are some very general rules that all human beings roughly accept, and which can form the basis for a common body of law, both personal and international. It is then possible to derive a series of general concepts relating to the environment. These are seen both from our general experience of natural law, and relate to our existence as "natural" creatures. They could be perhaps summed up in three colloquial phrases:

- Don't soil your own nest
- Don't spoil your offspring's future
- Take only what you need

Don't soil your own nest

In other words, be careful of your own mess, and don't let your rubbish accumulate and become a hazard. This is in part a recognition that most animals that live in closely-knit colonies seem to keep them relatively clean.[6] This is readily translated into a care for the disposal of the waste products from all human activities, such that they do not incur damage to the environment or to other living creatures in the environment.

Don't spoil your offspring's future

This is in many ways similar to the stewardship argument, in that it is unnatural to act in such a way as to create conditions that will make it difficult for one's offspring to survive and thrive. It can moreover only ever be a partially binding rule, for it is not reasonable (or natural) to expect any animal to refrain from eating, and so starving, on the grounds that the same food might be available to as yet unborn offspring. The maternal action of giving up food for ones offspring is however a common observation in nature.

Take only what you need

This is perhaps an elaboration of the first two: a call not to consume what it is unnecessary to consume. It is generally thought that most wild animals consume only what they need, and that only human beings and their pets will eat themselves into positions of life-threatening obesity. This can then be generalised to all sorts of non-food commodi-

---

[6]   Although we note that this is not an inevitable rule—some seabirds for instance live on great mounds of excrement, which we refer to as guano.

ties, and applied to issues such as mining, forestry, and land management in general.

These three rules are an attempt to identify some of the possible contents of a natural environmental law, taking its inspiration from the life of animals. It is equally possible to take other conclusions from the same source, and in particular take note of Tennyson's description of Nature as "Red in Tooth and Claw" (*In Memoriam*).[7] The observation that the fate of most organisms is short and violent, and most are likely to end up as a meal for another organism long before they can achieve maturity, can support the claim that Nature is essentially amoral—if not immoral. So many species (perhaps the majority) produce an enormous number of offspring so that one may survive. The "higher" animals are perhaps unique in this respect, only because they engage in a different strategy of protecting their young into adulthood. Everything can be seen in the endless cycle of "eat or be eaten".

Although the Victorians (such as Tennyson) could therefore see in Nature a chasm of chaos and conflict, it is also possible to see the same cycles of eating and being eaten as the way we all participate in the cycles of nature. We are part of the Nitrogen cycle, the Carbon cycle, and so on. The true purpose of humankind can thus be seen to maintain its place in the cycle of all materials and nutrients. This can be turned into an environmental ethic by arguing that humankind should not use any materials that they would not use in their natural condition—but this effectively means abandoning the whole of civilisation.

It is also possible to take the same observation, and argue that human beings are part of nature, and all that we do is natural, and so our cycling of all materials is in some sense natural. This might then be construed as giving ourselves carte blanche to do whatever we like in order to survive,

---

[7] Not all editions present the stanzas of *In Memoriam* in the same order. My edition, which gives the stanza quoted here as no 56, is *Poetical works of Alfred Lord Tennyson*, The Globe edition, Macmillan and co, London, 1928. (reprinted from the first edition in 1899). In it Stanza LVI is printed on page 261.

with concern for animals thus becoming a luxury the well off and well-protected can afford, not a moral imperative.

It is thus possible to note that an attempt to derive an environmental ethic from nature can be a difficult issue, with many people coming to different conclusions from the same starting points.

Chapter 4

The variety of approaches to environmental ethics

The central problem approaching environmental ethics is posed by the simple question, which is indeed the theme of this book: why should we protect the environment? There are many answers to this question, and that also is a central thesis of this book. Consequently, in order to develop the presentation of the many approaches, it is useful to structure the discussion by means of a classification. There are many ways such a classification can be approached, depending on the viewpoint and the concerns of the classifier. In this study, we will start our classification from the central question posed by Attfield (2003) who identified the problem as that of location of value in the environment. We will thus approach our discussion based on an increasingly strong valuation of the environment.

Other classifications are available, and offer their own insights. Particularly valuable is that offered by Dryzek (1997) from the study of politics. Dryzek's analysis offers an especially valuable insight, in that he characterises environmental groups as "discourse" groups, himself adopting an insight from linguistics. A "discourse" is a shared way of comprehending the world. The group that shares this understanding shares a common language, used in a special way. It is often based on a common analysis of what the problems and issues are, and the appropriate solutions. The group thus tends to become inward looking, conversing mainly within itself, developing an increasingly esoteric use of language, and conversing with other groups with increasing difficulty. This insight can be used irrespective of whether we follow Dryzek's own classification or another.

However, it is important to recognise that classifications are useful tools, not hard and fast boundaries, and it is possible to find environmentalists who appear to operate within various and varied locations within any classification, and also to recognise that the discourse groups so recognised are not hermetically sealed, and that individuals may converse with several groups. With that caveat, it is then possible to introduce the classifications themselves.

A political classification of environmental attitudes

Dryzek (1997) himself offers a two-way classification of discourse groups based on two criteria: reformist vs. radical and prosaic vs. imaginative, to give a simple classification table:

Table 1. A political classification of environmental discourses (Dryzek, 1997, p. 14)

	Reformist	**Radical**
Prosaic	Problem solving	Survivalism
Imaginative	Sustainability	Green Radicalism

Each of the entries in the table covers a wide range of groups, so it is possible to expand this table in many ways. Examining each of these areas in turn:

The *Prosaic Reformist* problem-solving approach is perhaps the world in which most environmental specialists have to work and live. It is based on the common picture of concerned governments or managers identifying environmental problems, and then seeking solutions to the problems. Depending on the viewpoint of the respondent, the answer to environmental problems can be identified by reference to one of three principle mechanisms.

(i)   The first and most common solution is to identify environmental problems as technical issues that require the attention of the technicians and specialists. The catch phrase is then "Leave it to the experts." The environment is thus an area where the public concern is expressed, if at all, through the actions of ministries and agencies, who identify and then seek to solve problems on behalf of the people who delegated the authority to them, and who seek to act on the advice of the experts brought in to identify solutions.

(ii) A second response to environmental issues is to evoke the operation of a truly free market. This response typifies those economists who advocate a free market for everything. In response to environmental problems, their reply is to assert that economic forces, if left to operate freely will resolve the problems, as those who wish to see certain environmental courses of actions will be prepared to pay for the benefit. Their response is thus "Leave it to the market."

(iii) A third response is to see many environmental problems as a consequence of a disassociation between the people and those acting on their behalves. As governments and their agencies become increasingly remote from those they govern, the ground swell is for more local democracy, and more local decision-making. Their answer to problems is "Leave it to the people."

We might wish to argue that in any situation, the issues are best resolved by a combination of these views, but in one sense they identify the three axes on which all governments act: the expert opinions of what ought to be done, the economic realities, and the wishes of the people. The extent to which various governments have in practice been able to act within these constraints has been illuminatingly described by Dryzek *et al.* (2003).

The *Prosaic Radicals* are those who identify an environmental crisis, but think that solutions should be based on current societies and structures. They can themselves be most simply subdivided into two main subgroups: Survivalists and Optimists.

(i)   Survivalists are those who observe the current situation in the world and see it heading for a non-survivable disaster. They see the gradually accelerating use of finite resources leading to a galloping crisis of resource exhaustion. A critical text is the classical "Limits to Growth" report to the Club of Rome (Meadows *et al*, 1972).

(ii)   The response to this is a "Promethean" optimism, which sees the only limits to growth being the ingenuity of humankind to solve its own problems. They are among those who see the environmental problems as being caused by technology, to which the answer is more and better technology.

This division into optimism and realism (pessimism) is noted elsewhere in the environmental debate: for example by Green (2000) and Small & Jollands (2006).

The *Imaginative Reformists*, in Dryzek's table, espouse the need for a complete re-structuring of modern society and economics, but feel this is best resolved by a process of gradual evolution and reformation. There are two strands to this movement: those whose key word is sustainability, and those who seek ecological modernisation.

(i)   Sustainability is a key concept that is discussed in Chapter 5, pp. 64–66 below. Its use came from the Developing World, where in particular agricultural projects were seen as either "sustainable" and hence capable of relatively limitless continuation, in that they did not use up non-renewable resources, nor led to degradation of the land; or else non-sustainable, and by leading to a rapid degradation of the natural resource, were essentially exploitative. The language of sustainability has moved into much wider use, and now applies to a wide variety of products and developments. The key concept remains, that the activity in question does not lead to a long-term degradation of resources or excessive use of non-renewable materials.

(ii) Ecological modernisation takes a rather broader approach, and sees the need for a thorough recasting of modern society, and the way it uses the environment. It differs from the more radical answers, in that it attempts to achieve the necessary changes through a process of evolution and argument, rather than a complete and sudden over-throw of the existing order. They are perhaps the realists compared to the idealists who suggest a new start. As such, they are not necessarily anti-technology, and see technology as helping, but not necessarily driving, the evolution of a new ecologically beneficial society.

The final group that Dryzek identifies, the *Imaginative Radicals*, are the most diverse group. The fundamental characteristic is that they see the current economic and social system as, in the long term, unsupportable. Where they differ is in terms of what new solutions they propose, and what they see as the reasons behind the current problems. All tend to adopt an anti-technology approach. Dryzek subdivides them into Romantics and Rationalists, depending on whether they appeal essentially to the emotions or the rational senses. However, this subdivision is perhaps less satisfactory than his others, as it is quite clear that no matter how rational it may seem, no approach can ever be adopted if it does not appeal to the heart. (This point is made by Clark, 1993, who argues that only a religious foundation would motivate people to make the sacrifices necessary in adopting a completely new life style.) This group includes The Deep Ecology movement, as well as green radicals, and some religious approaches to the environment. (These will be discussed in chapter 5.)

Problem solving or life style change?

One major distinction that needs to be carried forward to further discussions, is that between those on the top left and those on the bottom right of Dryzek's table. This distinguishes between the radicals, who see the current environmental crisis as requiring a change in the whole life-style of western culture, and those who see the same crisis as a problem to be fixed by the use of appropriate technology. This identifies a fundamental dichotomy between those who see the depth of the current crisis as requiring a complete change in life style, and those who see it as a problem to be solved by adjusting or evolving current life patterns. The division between the two groups is characterised by Arne Naess's distinction between "deep" and "shallow" ecology (Naess & Rothenberg, 1979).

The problem-solving camp is widely represented in western governments, and is perhaps the *modus operandi* for most government departments and agencies charged with a care for the environment. These departments tend to adopt an ethic and praxis that assumes that environmental problems are the result of technical imbalances in the current technological life style, which can then be corrected through the implementation of better science and technology. Their discourse community sees the main agents as benign and enlightened governments calling in teams of experts. They then set up ministries and agencies to give the experts the problems to solve, and then to implement the actions suggested by these same experts. They are often only nominally democratic, as the agencies are answerable only to an elected assembly, and hence often remote from the people whose lives they affect.

The opposing discourse groups are much more radical in their analysis. They call for complete changes in the lifestyle of western civilisation. Depending on their particular allegiance, they require changes to major parts of the western economy. Most want to see a reduction in the carbon-based energy consumption that has created the current climate change crisis. Many want a return to simpler life style. Opposing them, many see this approach as merely impractical dreaming.

A value classification of environmental positions

Rather than using the Dryzek classification, this book uses a classification of environmental positions by reference to the central issue identified by Attfield (2003) as that of location of value in the environment. We thus posit a classification along an axis of increasing strength of the valuation of the environment. Each person will adopt their own position on this axis, and indeed may be inconsistent in adopting a position, and can even adopt different positions for different aspects of the environment. We pose this classification in the form of a table:

Table 2. A Value based classification of Environmental positions.

	Environmental Value: Weak
1	No Value
2	Hedonism
3	Utilitarian
4	Consequentialist
5	Intrinsic
6	Extrinsic
7	Theistic
	Environmental Value: Strong

We will examine each of these stances in turn in the following chapter. The same axis also includes those who find no value in the environment, and this attitude will also be the subject of a brief initial examination. We also have to note that there are many components to the concept of value, and these are often used uncritically. Each of these versions of value will appear in different ways in the subject chapter, but it seems useful to identify some of them at this stage.

Many philosophers have, in the past, started from the notion that value requires a value-er—which effectively means human beings. The basic concept of value is thus the value that human beings put on another object or action. This leads immediately to the concept of *economic value*. This concept assumes that the way human beings operate is to use money to establish the value, and the operation of the market place to allocate the resources available to them. The market place is thus seen as the ideal (or idealized notional) location where people exchange their wealth for their needs and preferences. Of course, not all have the same wealth, nor the same needs, so there is always an element of privilege in the operation of the market place. The market place can also be used to allocate non-physical goods: for example it is clear that in general people are prepared to pay to move their residential location to a more pleasant from a less pleasant place. This observation is of course the sort of behaviour that we use to establish an economic valuation of environmental goods, discussed in Chapter 5, pp. 53–59. It can also be basis for other ways of allocating other preferences, for example in the consideration of risk. So, for example, Beck (1992) notes that we tend to use our economic privileges to reduce our exposure to risk, so creating the so-called "Risk Society" (Mythen, 2004).

Some also consider that the environment has an *intrinsic value*, independent of any human evaluation. How there can be such a value without a valuer is a subject of debate, but it is perhaps academic if we consider that the object of environmental ethics is to help human beings to decide how to behave. Discussions of the possible ways of interpreting the varieties of intrinsic values are given, *inter alia*, by Rolston (1994) and O'Neil (2003)

Yet other sorts of value can be identified. Of particular relevance is that of *moral value*, which defines the area of moral concern. If a thing or action has moral value, then it needs to be the subject of moral systems. This underlies the argument of Midgley (1983) where she concludes that Robinson Crusoe had duties to his island, and so by extension, we all have duties to the environment in which we find ourselves.

Other sorts of value can be devised, some of which may illuminate the issue of environmental ethics. What is clear is that many sorts of value, often only implicit, are in circulation among environmental groups. We need to be careful to accept that many of these are derived from conflicting or at least complementary bases and assumptions.

Chapter 5

Ways of valuing the environment

No value

Somewhat ironically, we start by examining the assertion that there is no immediate value in the environment. This is perhaps a default position: that the environment is of no interest to the human race, except as its location and its source of resources. This stance was perhaps that of the mediaeval Christian schoolmen, such as Aquinas, who saw the world as of little consequence, simply because of the over-riding concern of winning their way to heaven. Even such a bleak valuation is not without its implications for the environment, because under these conditions there is still the condition of being human. If we accept the bleak assessment of Hobbes (1651) that life is "solitary, poor, nasty, brutish, and short", then our aim in life must be to grab as much as we can for own enjoyment. In which case the argument for a concern for the environment grades gradually into the hedonistic category, as we try to capture and then look after those bits that please us; or else into the utilitarian argument that we need to husband the things that are useful, so that we may have the best use of them.

Most human beings, however, do not live by an ethic of utmost selfishness. At the least, they live as part of a family unit, and then as part of social groups: extended family, village, town, or nation. Under these conditions, they have some regard for their fellow human beings. Normally, the family ties are the strongest, but others are capable of strong motivation for behaviour. A common component of these social groups is the recognition of a common ethic, and a common concern for each other. Even if the focus of the concern is totally people-centred, it will still probably require some regard for the environment, both as a shared space, and as a shared resource. It is thus possible to argue that any normally constituted human being will have some concern for the environment as the spaces within which they live and in which they interact. It may be possible to claim no concern for the environment in the sense it is usually used now, but in the strict sense, such a claim is unlikely to be absolutely true.

Hedonist value

Hedonism, the pursuit of pleasure, would protect the environment, or portions of it, simply because we like it and enjoy it. There is nothing inherently wrong or demeaning about this attitude as far as it goes. Although many, perhaps most, accept that the simple pursuit of pleasure is not, on its own, the basis for a fulfilled life, it is a starting point for many activities. It is the basis of most human experience, that some things are pleasant, and other things less so. Consequently, we learn to seek the pleasant things, and the things we like, whilst avoiding those things that are harmful or unpleasant.

In the same way, as they grow, human beings learn to identify and name the environment around them. In doing this, they automatically begin to identify the things that give them pleasure, and the things that they do not like or harm them. Consequently, we find human beings will gather things round them that they like, and they will visit places they enjoy, and which have pleasant memories associated with them. Almost without thinking, the environment around us is subconsciously classified into things and places pleasant and unpleasant. On maturity, human beings become more responsible for arranging their immediate environment. They choose their dwelling places, and the modes of decoration, and so spend a lot of time and effort making their immediate environment acceptable and pleasant for themselves. Hence the market for interior designs! City planners and architects expend a lot of effort ensuring the urban environment is as interesting and pleasant as they can make it.

In modern urban life, concern for our environment extends beyond our immediate surrounds, to embrace the countryside and the wider world. Consequently, most modern city dwellers spend time and effort in accessing and admiring the rural and the wild environment. We can see this in the way urban dwellers head for the countryside for their holidays. Many seek rural locations to provide peace and quiet, and natural-ness, that is lacking in their urban lives. Many seek to retire there; others buy pictures of the countryside to decorate their dwellings. This then becomes part of the great urban dwellers' love affair with the countryside. It is always a moot point as to just how realistic the urban-dweller's vision of the countryside actually is. Inevitably it is coloured by the countless reproductions of works of art such as the paintings by Constable; the portrayal of country life on radio[1] and television; and a nostalgia for a lost past. However, even if this vision is unrealistic, it is still the source of much concern for the environment within the majority urban population. (See the essays in Barnett & Scruton, 1998). In political terms, the issue of realism is probably not important, until the debate becomes centred on issues where reality and vision conflict, of which the attitude to animals is a critical example. The liking for the natural environment thus probably underpins much of the tacit political consent for environmental protection from the majority of voters who no longer live in direct contact with it. Depending on the definitions used, the rural population of many western countries is no more than 10%. It is further clear that a larger silent majority seems to support moves to protect the environment. This is perhaps illustrated by the massive 15% of the votes gained by the UK Green Party in

---

[1]   In the UK *The Archers* radio programme is particularly influential.

the 1989 elections to the European Parliament, and the electoral success of the Green Party in Germany is also notable (Dryzek *et al.*, 2003). The same regard for the environment and its creatures can be observed in the current vogue for wildlife programmes on television, presented by high profile names, such as that of David Attenborough, supported by popular beautifully illustrated books (e.g. Attenborough, 1979; Richards & Tyabji, 2008).

It is also possible to observe that because we are ourselves part of nature, many of us love animals as part of that same whole. If the Earth is seen as a continuous whole, then human beings themselves are both part of it, and in some sort of relationship with all the other creatures and objects of the natural world. It is only as we grow, that we learn to distinguish categories of animals, and place boundaries between them and ourselves. Consequently, we often develop a concern for both animals and their environments as we come to appreciate our own natures. Therefore, we care for them and their part in the same ecosystems in which we live and flourish. The extension of the consciousness and regard to the wider environment is one of the key points of the Deep Ecology movement (see pp. 77–80).

Utilitarian value

Utilitarian ethics wishes to protect the environment because it is useful to human beings. Utility can thus be seen as the source of values including:

i.   The environment as a source of raw materials. This includes most of the materials for our life style—stones, metals, and energy.

ii. The environment as a potential source of new and useful substances. For example, tropical rain forests have been identified (and exploited) as sources of natural substances that might be used as drugs, flavours, or perfumes.

iii. The environment as a source of natural energy— although we also note nearly all attempts to use that energy involve interventions in the natural system that may be considered environmentally undesirable (dams and wind turbines for example).

iv. The environment as a resource of unused space that needs to be available for the expansion of human activities when required. Its value is thus defined by its potential that is being set aside for future use.

v. The environment as a place for recreation and refreshment in many ways for many people.

This list could probably be expanded to fill several pages, as we add together the possibilities, which would show that, for many reason, human beings find utility and hence value in their environment. By accepting the use of this value, the environment becomes capable of economic analysis.

The utilitarian analysis underlies the nub of the "Limits to Growth" report (Meadows *et al.*, 1972), and its concern for limits posed by continued usage of finite resources. Such a concern for the exhaustion of resources implies a consideration of the wish to carry on our existing activities into the future. It can then be further extended to the wish to pass those resources on to future generations in a state that will not excessively prejudice their use by those generations. This implied obligation to the future forms one basis for the concept of stewardship.

The challenge of an economic evaluation of the environment

The discipline of economics studies the way human beings allocate resources between and among themselves. Economists argue that this is best done by reference to the concept of value, and the operation of systems of markets, in which purchasing participants express their needs, their competing desires, and their willingness or ability to pay for, those resources. It can also be argued that this sort of valuation and trading system is widely used by human beings for many systems that are not in themselves inherently economic.

The most common way of attempting to establish a basis for institutional environmental decision-making is the modern utilitarian argument, which assumes that the environment is an economic good like any other, and that the way to deal with it is via the market place (see Turner, Pearce & Bateman, 1994, for a full length debate and defence of this assertion). The aim of such approaches is to put the environment onto a common basis with other variables. By giving the environment an economic value, it is then possible to compare it with other goods, similarly expressed, on a common basis. This view recommends itself to governments because it allows an apparently rational allocation of resources, and a way of reconciling conflicts on an objective basis using the familiar technique of cost benefit analysis.

This programme is not without its problems: the initial difficulty being that of putting a value to the environment, either in whole or in part. This problem of valuing non-economic goods is a major research area among economists. "Valuing natural goods is one of the major problems of ecological economics" (Klauer, 2000). Further, there are those who oppose the use of such methods outright, arguing that it is not only impossible to put value on the environment (and indeed other non-economic goods), but also actually wrong and confusing. Nevertheless, a number of standard ways of approaching the valuation of the environment can be identified, and economic valuation of the environment is by now a reasonably developed discipline (Foster, 1997). In Dryzek's terms, the community of economic evaluators has become its own discourse group, with its own worldview, its own terminology, and its own research problems and agenda. Typically, this group seeks to identify ways in which people are prepared to pay for the environment as a resource. There are a number of approaches to identifying this value, which include:

— Property price approach

This attempts to identify to the amount people are prepared to pay for access to the environment, in particular as reflected in the value of their properties. By comparing the value of similar properties in different environments, a value can be put on the environment itself. This of course requires a lot of care to make sure the values are not con-founded with other factors, notably the economic health of the locations. Parallel evaluations may be made for other ways in which purchase choices reflect environmental atti-tudes; the current vogue for "organic" foods is perhaps an example.

– Travel cost evaluation methods

This measures the amount of time and effort people are prepared to spend to visit a specific environmental location, and to use this as the measure of value. For example, Scarpa *et al.* (2000) have attempted to put a value on the inclusion of Nature Reserves in Forest systems by enumerating visits costs and frequencies. However, they had to use other approaches to define willingness to pay for facilities that do not yet exist.

– Political evaluation

It is also possible to evaluate the amount of cash that societ-ies as a whole are prepared to pay for environmental poli-cies. In this way, the actions of the state are identified as the collective expression of the whole. It may be expanded to include the budget of non-state environmental bodies. The amount of cash available in a political situation reflects many other issues, notably the available resource and the competing demands placed on it.

– Contingent Valuation method

Contingent Valuation (CV) is perhaps the most commonly adopted method for valuing environmental schemes. In it, people are asked how much they are prepared to pay to preserve the environment, or more typically a specific area or component of it. These questions are often asked in a questionnaire or in a group discussion forum, in which the respondents are asked to indicate how much they are pre-pared to pay (for example via taxes or other institutional revenue raising actions) to maintain or improve part or whole of the environment. Alternatively, people may also be asked how much (in money terms) they would want as compensation for a loss of a certain environmental good. In this way, research attempts to put monetary vales to environmental "goods" or "services" by identifying people's Willingness to Pay (WTP). The skill required by the researcher is to ask the relevant questions in a way that elicits a realistic answer. Faulty survey or questionnaire design can lead to anomalous results.

There is an almost an infinite number of objections to Contingent Valuation, the main ones being that people's reactions in these situations are in the first place unrealistic, and in the second place affected by their own social and financial backgrounds, not by the real value of the goods they are supposed to be valuing. It is thus often unclear what such methods measure, and in what respect the respondents reply: as individuals or as citizens, selfishly or unselfishly; whether they are really giving economic value or buying moral satisfaction. It is observed that in many cases, some of the respondents put enormously large values on the environment, which can severely skew the results, as a sort of "protest vote". On the same grounds, others may give a value of zero, claiming that the environment is priceless. It is often necessary to identify and remove such responses from the analysis. The whole issue of the best way to achieve a CV evaluation is thus the subject of on going debate among economists.

Another major consideration in CV studies is the size of the population relevant to the questionnaire. This is critical, as the average price that the respondents are prepared to pay is then multiplied by the relevant total population. If the population group is the whole nation, then very small sums multiplied by a very large number gives unrealistically large values, unless the question is applied to the whole environment. Additionally, it is normally assumed that when evaluating a specific site, the amount people are prepared to pay will diminish with their distance away from the site. The choice of the distance decay function is critical in giving realistic answers.

It has been reported that even in the open workshop situation, the participants can have great difficulty in putting values on environmental goods, even when those same participants have been well informed about the issues involved (Clark *et al.*, 2000). It was clear that the participants in the discussion reported by Clark *et al.* (2000) had put a lot of effort into the attempt to put a value on a Wetland Enhancement Scheme. However, most of those interviewed felt uncomfortable with the whole exercise; indeed some actually felt outraged that a monetary value was being sought for something they thought was beyond price. This is why Clark *et al.* gave for their paper title a quote from one of the respondents: "We struggled with this money business." A common thread in all the responses quoted is: "nature is beyond value". This is one, but only one, of the "protest responses" to CV surveys, and is counteracted by other studies that support the assumption of a generally positive attitude toward paying for public goods (e.g. Jorgensen *et al.*, 2001).

The problems of the Contingent Value method raised by Clark *et al.* (2000) may be easier to resolve in more concrete situations where monetary loss is an issue, such as flood alleviation schemes, or road improvement schemes, where loss of time and inconvenience are tangible problems that can be traded against the preservation of specific landscape areas. The method is thus perhaps best used where the issues are very specific. Thus, for example, Loomis *et al.* (2000) identified the willingness of participants to pay for specific "ecosystem services" such as water purification, erosion control, wastewater dilution, and recreation in a damaged riverine system (the South Platte river near Denver, Colorado). Where the issues can be reduced to such building blocks, then it becomes possible to use this method; but the use of the method for the wider issue of preserving whole ecosystems, as discussed by Clark *et al.* (2000) is less sure.

– Intrinsic value evaluation: ecosystem prices

Klauer (2000) presents an alternative, in which he attempts to identify the real value of ecosystems from information about the flows of material and energy within them. He then attempts to use standard economic models to develop a value of the ecosystem. This is an interesting approach, and may eventually yield to one valuation of intrinsic value, but it has yet to be developed to a usable metric. Adopting intrinsic (i.e. non-human) value is perhaps the point where most would argue that economic methods are no longer appropriate.

— Pragmatic considerations

However much we have doubts about the methods adopted, we are forced by sheer pragmatism to accept that governments and planners are swayed by such valuations, claiming they are "rational" ways of resolving arguments. In effect, by adopting any of the economic valuation methods, no matter how sophisticated they become technically, we are accepting the dominant utilitarian methodology. This point is discussed at some length by Foster (1997). Where there is a conflict, the issue often arises from different ethical stances, and so is not a technical matter between alternative ways of establishing the economic value of nature, but the issue as to whether nature should be so valued at all.

It is for this reason that many environmentalists are very wary of economists. Much damage has been done to the environment under the banner of economic progress. Consequently, when economists now attempt to include environmental goods in their analysis, are they (as Robin Grove-White, 1997, mischievously suggests) putting themselves "on the side of the angels," or are they just de-valuing nature by including it in the list of factors they are trying to evaluate and control? Economics is about the production, use, distribution, sale, and consumption, of goods. If we can treat the environment as a "good" then it becomes a legitimate subject for economic discussion and analysis. The decision as to whether we can make this identification is made outside the economic analysis, but lies in the "meta-economic" framework (Foster, 1997, quoting Schumacher, 1974), which we would identify here as the ethical framework. It is possible to accept a whole variety of such meta-economic frameworks. We can accept the utilitarian neo-orthodoxy that demands we use the tools of economics to resolve all issues of resource allocation, but we can adopt many other ways of putting values to the environment, as the various chapters of this book have identified. We must be careful to distinguish when we are making the challenge on such philosophical-ethical grounds. Most ethical systems find their values outside the realm of economic value theory; and to force the debate into the utilitarian framework is to wrongly identify the conflict. When the participants in Clark *et al.*'s (2000) discussion stated they "struggled with this money business", they were having difficulty not so much in allocating value, as in accepting the utilitarian framework.

Despite this, many countries, including the UK, have adopted the economic route and so established the rule that cost benefit analysis is to be used as the tool for evaluating environmental problems. This has been the cause of considerable frustration at events such as public enquiries, where the only issue that can be challenged by those opposing a development is the technicalities of the cost benefit analysis, not the use of this tool itself. The counter-argument to this and many arguments is that these ground rules are defined by a democratically elected government, as a matter of public policy, and that public enquiries are not the correct place to challenge that policy: that is the task of the elected chamber of parliament. This way of thinking, and the frustration it generates, is illustrated by the discussion of the Twyford Down case, described by Connelly & Smith (1999) and Bryant (1996).

Consequential value

Consequentialism focuses on our responsibility for the consequences of our own acts. In terms of environmental ethics, this means that we are responsible to others for what we do with the environment. If we destroy it, then it becomes unavailable to our children and grandchildren, or to our neighbours. A common theme in environmental ethics is that we are responsible to our successors. The common terminology used is that of stewardship—although this terminology is also and more properly used in the context of extrinsic valuation (see below, pp. 80–85). This terminology was, for example, used in one of the most famous speeches on the environment made by the then British Prime Minister, Margaret Thatcher, to the Royal Society in London, and repeated in her speech to the Conservative Party Conference in October 1984, when she said:

> No generation has a freehold on this Earth. All we have is a life tenancy—with a full repairing lease ... We are its guardians and trustees for generations to come.

In doing so, she launched the "greening" of the Conservative party, and the start of a *volte-face* that brought the environment from a position of exclusion to that of centrality in British government (Dryzek *et al.*, 2003). Parallel to this, the language of sustainability has also come into prominence in the last 20 years.

Stewardship

The language of Stewardship has many adherents, and has in many ways become the *de facto* terminology for looking after the environment. A classic statement is the "Eleventh Commandment" to be found in Lowdermilk (1953):

> Thou shalt inherit the Holy Earth as a faithful steward, conserving its resources and productivity from generation to generation. Thou shalt safeguard thy fields from soil erosion, thy living waters from drying up, thy forests from desolation, and protect thy hills from overgrazing by thy herds, that thy descendants may have abundance forever. If any shall fail in this stewardship of the land thy fruitful fields shall become sterile stony ground and wasting gullies, and thy descendants shall decrease and live in poverty or perish from off the face of the Earth.

The very language of this statement shows its origin as a paraphrase of Biblical material, and places it firmly within a Christian tradition. The concept of stewardship can also be found in many other contexts, and has over the last 50 years come to be an accepted secular definition of the relationship between human beings and their planet.

The basic notion behind stewardship is that we have a responsibility for the way we use our environment. The great discussion is to whom and how we are responsible. We can easily identify who these might be in human terms:

1.   *All human beings in the past,* who have passed the world to us in its current state. In particular, we think ourselves responsible to those who have worked to preserve beautiful parts of our landscape. In the UK, we might think specifically of those who established the National Trust and the National Parks. In the USA, we might think of people such as John Muir and the Sierra Club, who did so much to protect the Western Mountains. Equally, those who own and manage land will also think of the farmers before them, in many cases their direct forebears, who worked to make the land what it is today. In some situations, we are grateful for the hard work and care of previous owners, but in others, we might think of their efforts as problematical (as for example with previous generations of industrialists and miners who covered the land with toxic waste), and strive to correct their errors.

2.   *All other human beings currently on the planet*: our neighbours, our compatriots, and visitors to our own environment. This is an expression of the often-repeated observation that our obligations to our fellow human beings are not restricted by space. Consequently, we find arguments in favour of the global family of all human beings (or in older terms — the "Brotherhood of Man") to whom we are responsible for all our actions.

3.   *People yet to come.* We often say we wish to pass our land on to our children and grandchildren. We want to make sure they have the same enjoyment of the environment as we have; and so we wish to preserve, or even enhance it for them. It is difficult to see how we can have a relationship with people that we do not even know will exist — we cannot even predict how many great grandchildren we might have, if indeed any.

The big problem is establishing how such a responsibility to such nebulous groups of people might actually be expressed. The traditional language of stewardship implies a two-way responsibility and interaction, with the possibility of some resolution if the terms are broken or neglected. How this can be expressed cannot be immediately identified for any of these three cases. Even the second case, the responsibility to all our fellow human beings, cannot be sensibly invoked for people whom we will never know and with whom we will never interact. Only by the most global of actions can any one of us be said to affect the lives or expectations of others many thousands of miles away. We thus tend to consider this responsibility as being expressed through our interaction with people more adjacent to us. Consequently, we set up local rules and administrations, which express the overall stewardship ideal, but exercise it through local jurisdiction. This is the principle underlying much legislation: that international agreements (such as those governing the European Union, the Ramsar Convention on Wetlands, or the UN Declarations on the Environment) are implemented by the individual nation states through their own legal systems.

Responsibility to the past is even more difficult to envisage in transactional terms. We simply cannot interact with those who are already dead. Obligations to them are thus transmitted through the actions and structures of Society. Sometimes these are through organisations founded to carry on their work: the Sierra Club in the USA and the National Trust in the UK are examples, though there are now many more. Others are transmitted through society's memories and attitudes.

The same problem arises with transactional obligations to those yet to be born. We cannot know exactly who they will be, nor how many of them there will be. Although we can estimate numbers with a fair degree of accuracy through the use of statistical and demographic techniques, we cannot predict what disasters and chances will affect the make up of future populations. Consequently, we cannot enter a relationship with such people, nor can they ensure we act in a suitable way. The only retribution they can exact is to vilify our name retrospectively.

Consequently, all three categories of relationships are inevitably translated into current societal patterns: either societies' unwritten rules and expectations, or the rules and regulations that are their legal systems. This responsibility to the past and the future is thus part of the rationale for doing things in the present. We can pass legislation that, we hope, will protect the future, and we can act to correct the errors of the past, but we cannot know whether future generations will be grateful to us.

Similar arguments apply when we start to consider the issue of stewardship as a responsibility to other life forms on the planet, even to the planet itself. Ultimately, we may have to consider units larger than just the planet, even the Universe. Indeed, we might be said already to have some responsibility to the Moon and the planets, which are now littered with the remnants of our visits and explorations. Again, we might wish to say we have a responsibility to them, but this cannot be placed within any transactional framework, and again must be considered in terms of the current rules and structures of society.

Writing from a theological perspective, Palmer (1992) was particularly critical of the Stewardship concept, on two grounds:[2]

i. It is unduly focussed on the concept of money. The term was in use for some time before being applied to the environment, mainly in terms of financial resources, which were thought of to be husbanded, used wisely, and used to be grown for the future.

ii. It is a concept derived from inappropriate social structures. The notions of stewardship appear to derive from the historical use of the word, with the overtones of ownership and absolute obedience of the servant (steward); or from hierarchical models of the mediaeval monarch, which again

[2] Palmer also rejects the use as being non-Biblical, noting the Bible uses Stewardship only as an illustration not as a command to be followed.

implies ownership of the property being stewarded, and has hints even of the usage from the slave estates of the eighteenth century.

These objections suggest to Palmer that "stewardship" was a convenient label that was in vogue in the 1950s in other (notably financial) contexts, which was then adopted for use in a new context. She argues that a new term, free from some of the old associations would have been more appropriate. No alternative for the term stewardship has appeared, and it has now passed irrevocably into common usage. It has thus become part of the official language of the state; with the UK government for example labelling its current agri-environment grant scheme "Environmental Stewardship" (DEFRA, 2005). So despite the misgivings, as no alternative term has come into common usage, it seems that the language of Stewardship is irrevocably embedded in environmental language.

Sustainability

Sustainability has been used in many contexts, but has increasingly become the focus for much talk about land management. The many uses of the term are reviewed in Attfield (2003, chapter 6.) The language of sustainability has become important in four contexts: the use of resources, the agricultural context, the development context, and popular usage.

Sustainability is often used in the context of the management of resources, and is particularly used to suggest that resources need to be harboured and maintained. Even non-renewable resources can be used in a way that is described as sustainable, by implying that the current rate of consumption will not exhaust the supply, but can be sustained into the foreseeable future. Of course, no finite resource can be exploited forever, and there must therefore be a limit to the use of such resources. The mineral resources of the Earth are a classic example. However, it is possible to identify ways in which they can be used sufficiently slowly that future usage will not be excessively compromised by current consumption. It is reasonable to allow for technological advance that might replace critical resources in the future, or allow for identification of additional new locations of the resource, without blindly following the path of Promethean optimism.

Sustainability has also become an important word in the agricultural field. This use came to fore in the American context, following the experience of the dust-bowl years of the 1930s (see Lowdermilk, 1953). In this context, sustainability can be simply a technical issue: that of using the land correctly. It can then be seen in technical terms such as the adoption of correct cultivation practices to prevent erosion, the use of chemicals to maintain soil fertility, the appropriate use of machinery to prevent damage to soil structure, and so on. The term has thus come to cover a wider definition, and includes the use of the land system, even including both the wild life and the human life. Sustainable agricultural systems are thus seen as less intensive than current "industrial" agriculture, and may include traditional agricultural practices. It is also remarkably close to the "Land Ethic" of Leopold, which will be discussed in Chapter 5, pp. 75–77.

The third major use of the term sustainable is applied to Third World development. The term, sustainable development, was a central plank in the Brundtland report (World Commission on Environment and Development, 1987). The concepts behind it were in part a reaction against the big-project aid actions of the immediately post-colonial era. Typically, big dam and irrigation projects were seen as imperialism under another guise (Hayter, 1971), sometimes resulting in inappropriate, exploitative land uses. Sustainability concepts have thus been used to describe practices that are environmentally benign, and so avoid damaging consequences such as soil erosion and nutrient reduction. Sustainable agricultural systems are thus those that can continue indefinitely into the future, implying careful management of the soil and its fertility, and so are contrasted with high yielding but soil degrading systems. In many areas, the debate is linked with the debate about the continuation of traditional agricultural practices as

opposed to the adoption of western "industrial" agricultural systems (Blatz, 1994).

Sustainability is also a term that has recently appeared in
the market place. It is now commonplace to see items in the
supermarket labelled sustainable. The most frequent use is
related to wood and wood products. The market place
usage identifies wood as sustainable if the cutting
programme is matched with a comparable planting
programme, so the total woodland area is maintained.
There are many problems with defining and policing such
claims, and these are sometimes supported by external
evaluation (e.g. from trade organisations or governmental
accreditation). Some consumers, it appears, will be swayed
in the purchase decisions by these labels, and some organisations require this label from their suppliers. Similar labels
are also applied to paper and paper products, where they
may be used to describe recycled products.

Sustainability is thus a many-facetted term, which needs
to be used carefully. In particular, it is essential to know in
what way it is being used in any context.

Environmental rights

The intrinsic valuation of the environment identifies a value
in the environment, as a whole or a component of it, in its
own right, without reference to human beings. This leads to
positions such as animal rights, which identifies a right of
each animal to its own existence, or the right of the whole
ecosystem to carry on functioning without the interference
of human beings. If human beings interfere with the working of natural systems, they are in some respects interfering
with the rights of that system to continue their natural function and development.

The biggest problem of this viewpoint is then that of identifying the relevant rights and how those rights can be medi-
ated. All human actions in some sense violate natural rights,
so any sensible ethic has to decide at what point the viola-
tion is sufficient to require action. It also has to decide who
is responsible for monitoring and enforcing the rights of the

non-human world, since that world is inherently incapable of doing it for itself.

The language here is complicated, and contains at least two separate, though related, concepts that need to be considered: the Rights of Man and the Rights of Animals, and only then by extension to the rights of the wider environment.

The rights of man

The origin of the term "rights" comes from the language of the law. Initially rights was a legal term, in which one party gave rights to another party in exchange for some return action. For example, the mediaeval king could grant his barons the right to hold a portion of land, in return for which the baron would provide a fighting force derived from that land. The right was thus to enjoy the use of a portion of land, in return for which the baron undertook to provide the king with an army. Such a reciprocal relationship underlies many actions that convey rights, many of which now involve the transfer of money. Hence, rights are granted for payment, for example in the simple process of letting property. The rights themselves are defined clearly, and the payment terms identify the return action. Failure on behalf of either party to fulfil their obligations is a matter for legal redress. Rights are in this sense legally defined contractual terms.

More recently, a second usage of the term rights has evolved, which talks of the inherent rights of bodies. The language of rights gathered this extra dimension with the eighteenth century use of the phrase, the Rights of Man (the title of the extraordinarily influential book by Thomas Paine, 1791). Although the concept itself has its origins in the Greek concepts of Natural Law, its use was derived from the influential writings of John Locke and the events of the French Revolution (Almond, 1991). This new usage identified a number of rights that are intrinsic to all men (and by implication women) by virtue of their common humanity. This language became enshrined in the American Declaration of Independence of 1776, which states:

> We hold these truths to be self-evident, that all men are created equal, that they are endowed by their Creator with certain unalienable Rights, that among these are Life, Liberty and the pursuit of Happiness.

The subsequent, 1948, United Nations Declaration of Universal Human Rights, then states:

> All human beings are born free and equal in dignity and rights. They are endowed with reason and conscience and should act towards one another in a spirit of brotherhood. Everyone is entitled to all the rights and freedoms set forth in this Declaration, without distinction of any kind, such as race, colour, sex, language, religion, political or other opinion, national or social origin, property, birth or other status. Everyone has the right to life, liberty and security of person.

This language of rights has by now become the common ground for national and international debate (Almond, 1991) and is often enshrined in legislation. (For example, the UK law recognises the authority of the European Court of Human Rights.)

Such use of the term rights is however not uncontroversial. There are several issues that need to be resolved:

- First, it is not all clear where these rights originate. If, in response to the American Declaration of Independence, one were to say, "these rights are not at all self-evident to me", the discussion collapses. In current usage, it seems these rights are defined by common agreement, and so are close to the concepts of Natural Law. As they are normally given, as it were *ex cathedra*, and cannot then be debated, they are often treated with caution by those who derive their ethics from other bases, particularly those who see such rights as a challenge to an ethic revealed by divine action. Christian theologians, for example, tend to see such rights as irrelevant when compared to the revelation of the divine love for each human being.

- Second, it is far from clear how such rights are to be exercised or policed. Even assuming the rights are defined and agreed, there is no automatic guarantee that they will be respected. This is why it has been necessary to set up courts of Human Rights, and to translate their actions into legislation.

- Third, there are varieties of opinion as to what sort of beings can have rights. Initially the concept was applied to adult rational human beings: hence children and those with mental incapacity appeared to be excluded (although probably not intentionally so). Others have found rights in the capacity to suffer (notably Bentham, quoted by Singer, 1995 p. 7) and so include all human beings, including foetuses, and animals (but still excludes comatose humans, and perhaps foetuses in their early stages). The widest definition perhaps includes those who have an interest, but this is so wide as to include almost everything.

Despite the difficulties in defining the exact meaning of the term, the language of rights has become common parlance in many situations. A standard comic character is the awkward barrack-room lawyer who says, "I know my rights." Whereas this may be the common case for interactions between humans, it is less clear how it is to be applied to the environment. These are to be found first in the rights of animals, which are included in the Benthamite definition in being capable of suffering, and then in the even more contentious and nebulous concept of the rights of ecosystems and even the rights of the Earth.

Animal rights

A big debate has thus developed over the question of Animal Rights. This is to some degree independent of the parallel argument about cruelty to animals. The argument that animals have rights, similar to those of human beings, has been proposed, notably by Singer (1975).

Do animals have "rights": if so what are they, and against whom? Most philosophers base their discussion on rights on the terms of mutual inter-obligations, in which animals cannot have rights because they cannot reciprocate these obligations. Neverthless, there remains a residual thread within the philosophical literature that does indeed assert that animals have rights (see for example Singer, 1975, 1995 and Linzey, 1994 for a thorough review.) Singer (1995) follows the Bentham argument in identifying the capacity to suffer as the basis for rights. He argues that animals as sentient beings are capable of suffering, and that the capability for suffering is the vital characteristic that gives all beings equal rights. All sentient beings thus have equal rights to the avoidance of suffering. On this basis, we can construct an ethical basis for our relations with animals: that whatever we do to and with them, we must impose no more suffering on them than is absolutely necessary (for example, to protect ourselves).

The argument additionally raises other issues, such as the difference between suffering and feeling pain (are the two same?) and the degree to which animals lower down the chain (e.g. worms, bacteria, protozoa) can be said to suffer. This debate can become quite complex, when we move from the higher animals (notably the mammals that are our companions, and which appear quite clearly to suffer from problems such as neglect, maltreatment, or illness), to lower animals that appear to have only simple sensory organs and no apparent reaction to the expectation of pain. We accept here the argument that animals can feel pain in the way we do (a view that has been denied in the far past, when animals were considered to be qualitatively different from humans).

Rights based on the capacity to suffer is in fact a relatively wide view of rights, but one that has enormous practical consequences, because it admits of no boundaries in sentience. We therefore need to establish rules to distinguish between the competing rights of various elements of any situation. We note that Singer (1975, p. 21) accepts that it is possible to make decisions between the lives of animals and humans. What is important is that we accept the fact of the right of the animal to life, and lack of suffering. However, accepting that right does not negate the need to make choices about the life and death of ourselves and the living creatures of the natural world.

Environmental rights

It is possible to take the insight of animal rights, that rights are not the exclusive property of human beings, and then extend the application of the same language to the whole of the environment, and so attempt to identify Environmental Rights. These could then be used to imply that ecosystems have the right to flourish in their natural state, that geomorphological systems should be left to continue their actions without undue interference from humankind, and so on. We might even consider the Earth to have a right to continue without undue anthropogenic changes to its condition. (Although of course we must allow it to continue to change in response to its own geological situation: no system remains static over long time scales, so we cannot say that the Earth has the right to remain unchanged, only unchanged by our actions.)

All such discussions almost inevitably lead to the conclusion that the only just outcome is for the human race to abandon civilisation altogether, and go back to a prehistoric life-style. Such a conclusion may be logical (to some), but is totally unacceptable to most human beings, who would not want to abandon what they see as the benefits of civilisation, notably the value of scientific medicine. A few days living "back to nature" may be attractive to some, but not if it meant a life that is, in Hobbes's memorable assessment already quoted: "solitary, poor, nasty, brutish, and short".[3]

The same consideration can be inverted, by arguing that humankind's innate intelligence and skill are part of human nature, and hence part of the natural world, and consequently that all we see as civilisation is in fact an out-working of our natural gifts. This argument is incomplete, because human beings are also moral beings (Haslam, 2005), who do reflect on their actions and have consideration for the consequences of their actions. They thus seek to do what is right for themselves and for the environment – that is after all what this book is about.

Implementation of a rights ethic

The problem with any rights based ethics for non-human systems, no matter how defined, it that there is no route for

---

[3] I do not think it is a reasonable or an ethical suggestion that the human race should commit mass suicide!

the subject (animals, or ecosystems) to argue for their own rights, to agree to the terms of their use of the Earth, to accept the presence of human beings, or to enforce any rights that they might have. In every case, the rights of non-humans (and indeed some incompetent humans) must be implemented for them by agencies acting on their behalf. As a result, animal and environmental rights become legal definitions, to be enforced on behalf of the recipients by an agency that has been given powers to do this by society as a whole. Rights of non-humans thus become part of the way a society organises itself.

However, societies organise themselves and implement their preferences by many ways other than the passing of laws. There is thus strong moral dis-approbation for activities that are seen as inhumane to animals (such as beating dogs or horses) that are expressed at least as much by social pressures as much as by the law. Equally, non-governmental organisations express society's own wishes in ways that are parallel to the legal system. Consequently, there is in most nations, a plethora of organisations whose aim is to protect either specific groups of species (for example the Royal Society for the Protection of Birds), or environments (notably the county-based wildlife trusts). They work by a combination of indirect action (lobbying and publicity) and direct action (notably the creation of reserves). In the UK, the role of such organisations is analysed by Dwyer & Hodge (1996), and the progress recorded by Adams (2003).

The issues involved in animal rights also go beyond the environment, and embrace the contentious issue of the use of animals in scientific and other research (see e.g. Singer 1975; Gold, 1995; and Gatward, 2001). These authors raise many issues that are at least parallel with those raised in a consideration of the environment, but for which the answers may be different. The actions of the supporters (activists) may also be different, with the development of an extreme attitude that includes "direct action" against those who support the use of animals for experimental purposes. By contrast, environmental activists (eco-warriors) may disrupt environmentally undesirable schemes, but rarely target the individuals involved.

Environmental activism

The discussion has thus come to the point where we have identified "eco-warriors" and their actions. Such individuals (and sometimes organisations) act against, or in deliberate contravention of, the constraints of the law. The direct action of many people in mass protests against specific projects (notably big projects such as the building roads, airports, and power stations) has by now become a part of the environmental scene.

Often this sort of direct action arises out of frustration, in that the normal routes for protest and argument (such as public enquiries) seem to be totally biased in favour of those proposing the project. Such projects are often backed by a sponsoring government department, and benefit from the influence of powerful industrial lobbies that are backed by very large amounts of money and often appear to have considerable influence within the corridors of power. Consequently, the ordinary citizen often feels powerless in the face of a large juggernaught that will not be deflected from its intended project. The case of a road scheme project, that of the Twyford Down bypass, is particularly well documented by Bryant (1996), and illustrates how even the most politically aware, and relatively well funded protest fails in the face of a determined government department (see also the discussion of the same case by Connelly & Smith, 1999, pp. 112–117). Examples can be multiplied almost endlessly, but at least one case of success is documented by Perman (1973).

An alternative view is that the action of activists prevents or frustrates the legal actions of a democratically elected government. It can be argued that the choices made by such an elected government are themselves the actions of the governed, and that attempts to overturn such decisions are in fact anti-democratic. The protesters argue that such decisions are often made, not by the elected representatives, but by the powerful civil servants, technocrats, and bureaucrats, who continue their activities largely outside democratic scrutiny (see e.g. Tyme 1978).

Activists rarely achieve success in specific examples, but often make significant impacts on the overall programme. They claim "noisy defeats, quiet victories" which makes the proponents of such schemes more likely to tread with caution when a scheme is likely to receive public opposition. The question that each person has to resolve is whether such deliberate law breaking is justified to achieve a better overall environment. In a modern society, although ruled by law, this decision is by no means obvious, and the fact that many people come to different conclusions is itself an indication of the depth of the debate.

Intrinsic value

A much wider appreciation of the value of the environment is found among those who consider the environment as having not rights, but value of itself. To them, the environment does not have value for any human reasons (e.g. utility), but has its own intrinsic value, independently of any human valuation. That this value cannot be expressed in economic terms is thought to be self-evident, as there is no commonly agreed way of accounting intrinsic environmental value. Klauer (2000) for example attempted to identify value in terms of carbon, energy and information flows, and others have sought value in terms of biodiversity, but these are still research ideas, and not yet worked out in practical cases. The intrinsic value of nature is thus most frequently seen in opposition to the utilitarian valuation, which defines things in relation to their value to human beings. Such a utilitarian valuation may be the limit of the science of economics, but it does not fully exhaust the usage of the term value (O'Neil, 2003).

Considering intrinsic value in the environment makes the big step of accepting that it is morally considerable (i.e. requiring moral consideration). This involves the philosopher in moving away from the "human chauvinism" of classical ethics (Routley & Routley, 1979) and morality, which considered the issue of morals as arising from trans-actions between independent rational units. Midgley (1983) observes that the classical model of the social contract makes just this assumption, drawing its model from seventeenth century (Cartesian) physics. She observes that the morality we live by certainly does not accept the restriction to fully rational adult humans, and that descriptions of ethics drawn from such premises are in need of an urgent update. There are indeed several ethical systems that can be offered as alternatives. Some have already been discussed. The two that fall most immediately in this category are the Land Ethic, and Deep Ecology.

The land ethic

A popular approach to thinking about the environment is the justly famous chapter: "The Land Ethic" in *A Sand County Almanac of Aldo Leopold* (1949, and reprinted many times, e.g. in Gruen & Jamieson, 1994, and Light & Rolston, 2003). In this chapter, Leopold proposed a "land ethic" that has become the basis of much recent discussion. Leopold's land ethic first extends the boundary of our moral concern to the community in which we function that includes "soils, water, plants, and animals, or collectively: the land". It turns human beings from conquerors to members of the land community. Leopold's description of the whole land system as the object of moral consideration thus resonates with the ecofeminist adoption of the holistic viewpoint.

The land ethic is stated simply: "A thing is right when it tends to preserve the integrity, stability and beauty of the biotic community. It is wrong when it tends otherwise." This short statement however needs much amplification before it can be put to practical use.

Subsequently, the land ethic has been widely adopted and developed by several American writers, notably among them Holmes Rolston III and J.Baird Callicot (e.g. Rolston, 1988; Callicot, 1989, 1999 & 2001). They place Leopold's ideas within the context of the Darwinian view-point, suggesting that Leopold's land ethic was an evolutionary development of existing human social ethics.

Sylvan (1973) used Leopold's approach as the starting point for developing a new environmental ethic. A common problem for all such "naturalistic" ethics, is to develop a criterion for choosing between the needs of each of the components of the system, and in particular choosing between the needs of humans and the needs of the natural system. In order to be practical, an ethic needs to be able to resolve such issues, and this is now an active area of discussion. It is in many ways a repeat of the same argument raised by the implications of giving rights to some or all parts of the ecosystem.

Callicot (2001) acknowledges the problem of pluralism in our ethical responsibilities in the holistic view of the Land ethic, and so identifies what he calls Second Order Principles that enable us to make decisions between the competing demands of our membership of multiple communities (social and Earth communities). These are: SOP-1: "Obligations generated by membership in more venerable and intimate communities take precedent over those generated in more recently engaged and impersonal communities"; and SOP-2: "Stronger interests generate duties that take precedent over duties generated by weaker interests". These do much to allow human beings to operate with the land ethic, without succumbing to the danger of self-righteous "eco-fascism".

One argument against this ethic is that it elevates a system—the ecosystem, or the land, to an object of moral consideration. It is not at all clear that this is permissible. When we allow value to the individual components of the land, animals, plants, rocks, these are things that can be identified and located. An ecosystem is a more nebulous identity, possibly only a concept useful to arrange and organise our thoughts. If it is not a thing in the concrete sense, it cannot (according to some) be an object for moral consideration. Whilst there is a need to answer this consideration, there is at the same time a widespread feeling that in identifying the land as the location for our concern, Leopold identified a real focus for our moral lives. Perhaps here our own moral lives are in advance of our philosophical thinking.

Because Leopold, and most of his adherents, come from the economically privileged American perspective, his advocacy of a return to naturalism cannot perhaps be implemented even in America. More fundamentally, it fails to recognise the link between environmental degradation and the plight of the world's poor. To resolve that issue, a more radical viewpoint needs to be developed (Smith, 1997).

Leopold was writing at a time when "ecology" was strictly an academic term, and the concept of an ecosystem largely unknown. (The background to, and the historical development of, his writings is explored in Smith, 1997.) In using the term "Land," he was writing about what we see and experience in the natural world. Land may be a difficult term to describe scientifically, but it resonates with basic human experience in a way that has given much power to the "land ethic".

Despite the problems of converting it into real decisions, Leopold's land ethic has received wide acceptance, particularly among conservationists: after all Leopold was a conservationist writing for other conservationists, and not a professional philosopher. Its simple formulation, and its alternative to a merely utilitarian view of the land is a down-to-Earth crystallisation of many trends of the previous century (Brennan, 2001) that has obviously resonated within the conservationist community.

Deep Ecology

In contrast to Leopold's land ethic, the Deep Ecology movement adopts a totally radical approach to the environment. It sees human beings as part of a greater whole, and the development of human awareness of its place in that greater whole as a process of self-realisation. This philosophy comes from the writings of the Norwegian philosopher Arne Naess, who describes it as "EcosophyT" — the term ecosophy being a contraction of Ecology and Philosophy, and the postscript T denoting that he developed it in the context of a specific place, his Norwegian cabin and retreat, Tvergastein. The point that any philosophy comes from the experience of living in a specific place or places, is well made and is well worth remembering.[4]

One starting point for a discussion of Deep Ecology can found in Naess & Rothenberg, (1989, p. 29), who present the "Platform of the Deep Ecology movement".[5] It both defines the movement, and illustrates the consequences of a intrinsic valuation of nature:

(1)   The flourishing of human and non-human life on Earth has intrinsic value. The value of non-human life forms is independent of the usefulness these may have for narrow human purposes.

(2)   Richness and diversity of life forms are values in themselves and contribute to the flourishing of human and non-human life on Earth.

(3)   Humans have no right to reduce this richness and diversity except to satisfy vital needs.

(4)   Present human interference with the non-human world is excessive, and the situation is rapidly worsening.

(5)   The flourishing of human life and cultures is compatible with a substantial decrease of the human population. The flourishing of non-human life requires such a decrease.

(6)   Significant change of life conditions for the better requires change in policies. These affect basic economic, technological, and ideological structures.

(7)   The ideological change is mainly that of appreciating *life quality* (dwelling in situations of intrinsic value) rather than adhering to high standards of

[4]   My own philosophy is thus tied up with my origins in the UK, and the environment there. I explicitly acknowledge this in Armstrong (2006 and 2007), and should perhaps suffix it with the initials BR, from the village where I currently live, Brompton Ralph, but that is to labour the point unnecessarily.

[5]   Naess identifies George Sessions as co-author of this platform. The text itself dates from the early 1980s, and has been much reprinted.

living. There will be a profound awareness of the difference between big and great.

(8)   Those who subscribe to the forgoing points have an obligation directly or indirectly to participate in the attempt to implement the necessary changes.

This platform is a rich text, and many things can be derived and argued from it. Among the points, it is observable that the initial statements (1–3) of the value of the non-human world appear without justification, as a given, in much the same way as the statement of human rights appears in the UN Declaration (see above, p. 68), and like the human rights, the whole structure falls if this basic ex cathedra tenet is rejected. Naess's statements (4–7) then move on to an analysis of the situation and the kind of action that is necessary to meet the aims of restoring the value of nature identified in statements 2 and 3. An even bigger jump is then contained within statement 8, which asserts an obligation for human beings to act: a jump that converts these statements from an academic analysis to an ethical proposition. Naess's programme also includes a statement that is rare among environmentalists: that a fundamental problem of the present time is the magnitude of the world human population.

The Deep Ecology position can also include a further dimension of self-identification (or self-realisation) with the natural world (Mathews, 1991). Here, the emphasis is not on the intrinsic value of the universe, but on the human self-realisation that springs out of "ecological consciousness". This version of self-realisation requires recognition of our place in an interconnected universe, and the expansion of our self-love to embrace the whole of that universe. It then requires the universe to have a self-hood, possessed of its own grand purposes and its own intrinsic worth. This expansion of our love to the whole of the world, thus gives meaningfulness to our own lives. The result is a cosmology and spirituality that is (it is claimed) close to that of many primal peoples, who do indeed identify themselves with the Earth and their locations within it. Mathews (1991) asserts that this "leap-inducing affirmativeness, which in its wider dimensions constitutes our spirituality, is innate to us". Ultimately then, Deep Ecology in this full sense, is a spiritual orientation, and so it should perhaps be best identified with the religious understanding of environmental value that we explore in the next section

Extrinsic value

Many ethical positions derive their stances from an external point of reference. This is normally some revealed set of teachings, either from a particular teacher, or more often from a religious standpoint. Indeed, socially speaking, one of the functions of religion is to teach and reinforce systems of behaviour.

The most common religious argument for caring for the environment is expressed in terms of a human responsibility to the creator God. This theme is common to the Judaeo-Christian tradition, the Islamic tradition, and many of the other world religions that think in terms of gods or a God. However, the acceptance of a religion does not necessarily entail an environmental ethic, as the relationship between god and humanity and the Earth varies between religions, and indeed within religions. Some religions regard the Earth itself as sacred, but this rather different viewpoint, is considered in the next section (pp. 86–88). The consequences of treating the Earth as the creation of a creator also vary between and within religions. These will be illustrated here by a discussion of the Christian tradition. Studies of other religious traditions have been noted in Chapter 2, pp. 11–15.

The Christian tradition

Both the Christian and the Jewish traditions have a long history both of concern for, and indifference to, the Earth. It includes not only a concern for the created order as the work of its creator, but also an indifference to this world in an over-riding concern for the next.

In the Old Testament, there is a very real concern for the land. The ancient Israelites were an agricultural race on the edge of the desert. Survival depended on the careful husbanding of resources; the careful use of what was available. Many of the aspects of their life depended on the appearance or non-appearance of the erratic rainfall, which could be, and sometimes was, interpreted as a sign of God's favour or disfavour. As a result, much of the prophetic literature in the Old Testament is couched in terms of agricultural plenty. So there are for example injunctions to let the land rest every seventh year. This could of course be seen as the translation into religious language of the simple practice of fallowing. It can also be interpreted as a non-exploitative attitude that cared for the land as part of their inheritance.

Barton (1998) argues that the Old Testament ethical material is carried as much by its narrative as it is by its apparently self-contradictory systems of rules, picking up the theme of Nussbaum (1986) who finds similar ethical content to the narratives of ancient Greece. The story of Naboth's Vineyard, to be found in 1 Kings 21, for example, is revealing, in showing the way the ancient Israelites saw their land, and its gifts as granted by God, and not to be sold or traded. In this way, we can see the way that the whole of the strand of the Old Testament that talks of the Promised Land as a land "flowing with milk and honey" has before it a vision of a harmonious relationship between the inhabitants and the land they occupied.

The New Testament is a little less explicit on its attitude to the environment, being more immediately concerned with the need to relate its experience of Jesus and his impact on the lives of those who knew him. Nevertheless, there are two clear indications in the New Testament. First, many of Jesus' tales, his parables, relate to the environment around him. Jesus sees, and apparently delights in his surroundings; sparrows, flowers of the field, the growing grain, among them. Second, the letters of St Paul see the redemption not just of the human race, but also of the whole world. Salvation is thus not just for human beings, but also for the whole Earth human and non-human, animate and inanimate. However, the early Christian tradition submerged much of its concern for the real world in its concern to survive. Under persecution, it became a private religion of personal commitment and holiness, not a religion of concern for the public good.

The emphasis on inner holiness, the need to attain salvation, remained the cornerstone of Christian thinking. Hence, Aquinas was concerned to see human life on Earth as a preparation for eternity. What was important was salvation, eternal life, and all else was subordinate to this eschatological aim. In that scheme, the whole of the non-human world is delegated to a means of attaining the necessary spiritual state of salvation. This strand is alive, so it is still possible to find a discussion that asks whether the Earth is our home or a hotel, somewhere we belong, or merely a staging post on our way to heaven (e.g. Murphy, 1989).

The critique of Christianity

In a famous address to the American Society for the Advancement of Science, in December 1966, Lynn White, a distinguished scholar, who at the time was Professor of Mediaeval History in Los Angeles, delivered a diagnosis of what he called the "Historical Roots our Ecological Crisis" in which he quite clearly placed the blame on Christianity (White 1967). The roots, he claimed, of our crisis, are the consequence of Christian theology.

> Modern science is at least partly to be explained as an Occidental, voluntarist realisation of the Christian dogma of man's transcendence of, and rightful mastery over, nature (White, 1967).

Science and technology, White argues, which are the reason for our current ecological crisis, are essentially the product of Western European culture, which is also intrinsically Christian. He argues the link between the two is clear and obvious, and has led to the current situation. He identifies two parts of the Christian doctrine that have lead to the problem:

i.   First that Christianity "desacralises" nature. It
     separates the creation from its creator, so it is
     possible to investigate the natural world without
     offending its gods. "By destroying pagan animism,
     Christianity made it possible to exploit nature in a
     mood of indifference to the feeling of natural
     objects" (White, 1967).

ii. Second, White argues that Christians derived
     from Genesis a view of the world in which the
     human race was seen as the culmination of
     creation, a different kind of being. In Genesis 1.28
     we read: "And God blessed them [the man and
     the woman] and God said to them, 'be fruitful
     and multiply, and fill the Earth and subdue it; and
     have dominion over the fish of the sea and over
     the birds of the air and over the every living thing
     that moves upon the Earth'". From it, he argues,
     we have taken the notion of dominion to excess,
     and so consider creation a resource to be plun-
     dered at will, by a dominant race whose home is
     in heaven and not really here on Earth.

There may of course be an element of truth in the argument,
but, then, Christianity has at one time or another been
blamed for almost every facet and ill of modern Western
society. For example, we have the famous analysis of the
historian R.H.Tawney (1926), who saw a link between Capitalism and Calvinist attitudes to work; Marx clearly saw a
link between the Christian church and the evils of society;
and Hooykaas (1972) has argued that it was only because of
the liberating attitude of Christianity, that science as we
know it had become possible. The easy identification of the
link between technology and religion has also been challenged, for example by Moncrief (1970), and others have
argued that Christian thought has always encompassed a
deep respect for creation (Attfield, 1991).

   In an important sense, White was right in recognising the
spiritual and religious dimensions of the present crisis. The
will to deal with our environmental problems cannot be
generated from anything except a religious understanding
(a point made with some force by Clark, 1993). The roots of

our ecological crisis rest in the way we look at our environment, how we, the current generation of *Homo sapiens* (a
misnomer if ever there was one), see our place in the scheme
of this world. White was also correct in identifying the roots
of the crisis in our culture. There is probably little doubt
among environmentalists that our prevailing cultural attitudes are in many ways inimical to the environment.

   In response to the criticism of Lynn White, a number of
alternative "ecological Christianities" have emerged over
the last few years. There are several possible insights that
serve as suggestions for a modern Christian theology:

- Based on a reflection on the incarnation,[6] or

- Based on the love of God for his Creation.

Both of these place a value on the environment that arises
from its relationship with God (see e.g. McFague, 1997). The
relationship of the creation with its creator gives it a value
that is thus intrinsic and completely external to the human
valuation. As such, they exemplify the environmental ethics based on an external reference point.

Consequences of an extrinsic evaluation of the environment

Adopting an external reference point for an environmental
ethic is, therefore, capable of a variety of interpretations. We
have already noted that some interpretations of the religious theme can lead to exploitative or indifferent attitudes
to the environment, but it is also possible to identify a number of responses to the religious vision that align themselves
with environmental concerns.

   The most common response is to identify the religious
viewpoint with the concept of stewardship. This seemed a
natural progression for many Christians who were using
the concept of stewardship for their own resource management (Palmer, 1992). It becomes easy to identify the absentee landlord/owner of the stewardship model with creator
God. In this view, we are then responsible to the creator God
for the use we make of the Earth, and for the condition in

---

[6]   The belief that God, in the person of Jesus, becomes part of his
      creation by being born as a human being within it.

which we hand it on to our descendants. The conundrum with the stewardship model, which is the problem of to whom are we responsible is thus resolved. However, it fails to give full weight to the Christian understanding of an immanent[7] God, who is far from being an absentee land-lord, and is instead continuously involved with his people and his creation. Despite this, the Christian background to the notion of stewardship is a widely used background to environmental discussion.

Alternative interpretations of the Christian vision can lead to an understanding of the environment very similar to that of the Naess's Deep Ecology. This is based on the Christian understanding of the whole of creation as having value, solely because of its relationship with God, and so worthy of our respect and care. It is, however, not necessarily the case that the whole of Naess's "Deep Ecology platform" automatically follows from this identification.

A more specifically Christian response to the environment can perhaps be seen in the suggestion of McFague (1997), who argues that the Christian practice of loving God and neighbour should be extended to nature. Consequently, she argues, we should relate to entities in nature in the same basic way that we are supposed to relate to God and other people — as ends, not means, and as subjects valuable in themselves, for themselves. She further argues that the Biblical "bias to the poor" elevates the need to protect the defenceless environment to a priority for all Christians. Nature becomes the new "poor", and so now demands our love, as do the human oppressed.

Theistic Earth ethics

A development of the religious dimension is to see the Earth itself as holy, and so to be venerated and protected because of that understanding. It can be specifically separated from the Christian and other religions that identify the Earth as a

---

[7] Immanence stresses God's dwelling in, and involvement with, creation, as opposed to his transcendance above creation (see MacQuarrie, 1983).

creation of a creator god, whereas the inherently theistic viewpoint locates the god within the created order itself.

This is perhaps the viewpoint of many of the native religions to be found around the world, which appear to talk consistently about the spirit of various parts of the environment, or indeed of the whole world. It can also be identified instantly but unhelpfully with the pagan idols that were the object of such horror by early Christian writers. More recent understanding of indigenous religious attitudes, values the identification of people with place, knowledge, and land (Whitt *et al.*, 2001). To them, the people and the land they live in are a continuous whole, in which the genealogical bonds provide the people with a sense of belonging not only to the land but also to its creatures and plants. These are explored in a series of extracts in Chapter 6 of Botzler and Armstrong (1998). Among them, Momaday (1998) expresses his relation to the land in the following way:

> Inasmuch as I am in the land, it is appropriate that I should affirm myself in the spirit of the land. I shall celebrate my life in the world and the world in my life. In the natural order, man invests himself in the landscape and at the same time incorporates the landscape into his own most fundamental experience. This trust is sacred.

This broad spiritual identification of people with the land they live in has been proposed as a paradigm for a new environmental ethic. It is difficult to see how it could be a practicable proposition for modern civilisation. To achieve it would require a degree of non-mobility that modern society has long since abandoned. Like much else in the environmental movement, it is in danger of becoming sentimental nostalgia for a by-gone age.

Modern theism: Gaia

A modern version of the theistic argument is given, at least in part, by James Lovelock's concept of Gaia (Lovelock, 1977 and 1988, and many more). The Gaia concept contains a mixture of mainstream science, speculative hypotheses, and spiritual aspiration (Kirchner, 2002). Despite the fact that it was written by a scientist, who claimed that he had no idea he was writing a religious book,[8] the Gaia hypothesis has taken on a quasi-religious significance among some of its followers. The personified Earth, which he describes as in some sense alive, has taken on a religious dimension among its followers,[9] and Lovelock has subsequently acknowledged this religious dimension:

> On Earth she is the source of life everlasting and is alive now; she gave birth to humankind and we are part of her. This is why for me, Gaia is a religious as well as a scientific concept (Lovelock, 1988, p. 206).

Lovelock describes the Earth system as capable of maintaining its own thermal equilibrium within narrow bounds despite considerable variations in the external conditions (specifically solar radiation). Such homeostatic behaviour is often considered a characteristic of life; and in this sense, Gaia could be thought of as alive. Lovelock also describes how Gaia might deal with irritants in her system, notably troublesome human beings. He ends up giving a warning that if we humans disturb the thermal equilibrium of our mother Earth, then she will get rid of the irritant. This could be seen merely as a utilitarian argument: if we upset the Earth's thermal balance, then we might expect our environment to become incapable of providing our needs. It can also be seen as a quasi-religious injunction to care for the goddess Gaia, who will otherwise be angry with us:

> Gaia, as I see her, is no doting mother tolerant of our misdemeanours, nor is she some fragile and delicate damsel in danger from brutal mankind. She is stern and tough, always keeping the world warm and comfortable for those who obey the rules, but ruthless in her destruction of those who transgress. Her unconscious goal is a planet fit for life. If humans stand in the way, we shall be eliminated (Lovelock, 1988, p. 212).

The practical consequences of this belief, in terms of action, are similar to those derived from most other mainstream

---

[8]   The claim is made by Lovelock in his 1988 book: "When I wrote the first book about Gaia I had no inkling that it would be taken as a religious book" (Lovelock, 1988, p. 203).

[9]   Many of whom claim the adherence to the Gaia myth on the mistaken grounds that it is a scientific theory.

analyses: we need to maintain the Earth in a state suitable for life. At present, we have nowhere else to go (although Lovelock does discuss the future possibility of a diaspora to the planets). In the practical sense, the consequence of a religion of a complete Earth system is not very different from the utilitarian analysis. It differs mainly in terms of motivation, and perhaps in terms of the amount of action that could be taken. Clark (1993) has argued that the degree of sacrifice necessary to reverse the current trends of Western civilisation could only be motivated by religious fervour. Perhaps Gaia could provide that motivation, but then so too could other religions!

Chapter 6

Praxis: Environmental ethics in practice

This review has considered the varieties of ways we can view the environment, and the variety of motives we bring to it. No matter how we classify the various streams of environmental concern, whether in the political terms of Dryzek, or the valuation axis (Table 2 on p. 423) used for this book, the conclusion is inevitable that people are concerned for the environment for many different reasons. If we accept the Dryzek (1997) analysis that each environmental position can be seen as a discourse group, then we become aware that these different groups may have difficulty interacting. However, environmental ethics is not an abstract discussion, carried out in the quiet of academia, but a very practical issue, debated time and time again whenever people engage with the issues concerning their environment. The issues that have been raised so far all have an impact on the way we approach real issues. This chapter looks at a few examples that raise these issues.

Democracy

We live in a small and overcrowded planet, and we cannot all have our way all of the time. We learn this at an early age, and we also at the same time learn that we have to live and work within the majority view of those around us. Consequently, we have to accept that environmental issues will be

resolved by some sort of negotiation process leading to
compromise solutions. This is the inevitable state of human
social life. Environmentalists need to be able to enter
debates about the environment. In doing so, they will need
to be able to see the way that their opponents think, both to
give them the courtesy to understand them, and in order to
be able to counter their arguments. Consequently, we need
to be able to identify all the players in each discussion, and
the bases for their concern. It will also be necessary to work
for the full discussion of environmental issues. Often those
with interests will try to avoid such discussion. The bureau-
cratic and technocratic mind-sets are particularly prone to
assuming that their answers (administrative or technological) are automatically right. Consequently, it is essential to
identify the relevant forums for these discussions.

It soon becomes clear that in many countries there is often
a shortage of relevant forums for the discussion at the
appropriate levels. Often decisions are taken by executive
bodies far removed from those who are affected by the decision. A classic case in the UK, described by Purseglove
(1989, pp. 244–58) is that of the Somerset Levels in the early
1980s. The issue was decided when the Secretary of State for
the Environment confirmed the action of the Nature Con-
servancy Council in designating West Sedgemoor as a Site
of Special Scientific Interest. This rather esoteric decision,
taken between government agencies, and hidden in the corridors of power at Westminster, was about as far away from
local democracy as it is possible to be in the UK. Following
this experience, there has been a recent development of
local democratic bodies, both independent and within the
framework of local government organisations, that have
generated a greater degree of local discussion and interaction (Armstrong & Bradley, 2007). The lessons from this
particular incident are that democratic processes need to be
undertaken at the right scale, and in the right place. Indeed
much of the anger reported by Purseglove (1989) was
expressed by local farmers at what they saw as undue interference from faceless bureaucrats from Whitehall.

Recreating nature

A fundamental decision needs to be made whenever human beings attempt to create or re-create Natural systems: to intervene, or to leave things to natural processes. This is particularly an issue when the proposal is to return an area to a "Natural" condition. This sort of requirement occurs quite frequently, and is often related to issues of government action and opportunity, particularly agri-environmental schemes (Armstrong *et al.*, 1995). An example to be found in the recent European legislation, is the Water Directive (EU, 2000). This directive sets out target conditions for water bodies throughout Europe, in which the target for High Ecological Status is nearly always expressed as "undisturbed conditions".

Consequently, there is a current movement to allow large areas to return to some sort of natural condition. (In the UK this is described and analysed in some detail by Dwyer & Hodge, 1996.) A wide variety of bodies, with varying aims, now manage land for conservation purposes: some to preserve an existing landscape; others to create or recreate natural areas *in toto*, others to manage land for specific components of the ecosystem (bird reserves are the commonest example).

The subject of natural recreation has been reviewed from the philosophical angle by Elliot (1982), who argues that even if perfect restoration were possible (what he terms the "restoration thesis" — I would prefer the term "restoration hypothesis"), some value is lost from the ecosystem, which is associated with its origins. The value we place on any environment almost inevitably includes some consideration of its origin, and it is both reasonable and intuitive to consider an undisturbed system to be of greater value because of its pristine state. A restoration is thus to some extent a "fake", which is therefore inherently less valuable.

In restoration/recreation projects, a major problem is that for large areas of Europe (nearly all the UK for example) undisturbed conditions have long since disappeared. In many areas, an attempt to return to a pre-anthropic state means reversion to a time, perhaps as much as 5000 years ago when the climate was significantly different from current conditions (even ignoring the current anthropogenic climate changes), and in many geomorphologically active areas the landforms have changed. In the North Sea coastal areas, for example, where geomorphological changes associated with variations in sea level have been dramatic, it is no longer possible to return to an historical status.[1] The consequence is that, even if it were to be a correct aim, it is in many places difficult, or even impossible, to identify a pre-anthropic state that could be the object of an historical re-creation. In the majority of circumstances, a return to an historically reconstructed past (even assuming it could actually be sufficiently precisely defined) and its re-creation is just not possible. The aim of such re-naturalisation projects will require instead the definition of a new target ecosystem, which is the one that we chose to create. This places decision makers in the much more difficult situation of having to make a positive choice about the kind of ecosystem they want to create.

In all re-naturalisation projects, after the choice of aims, the next biggest decision is to identify the degree of anthropic intervention that is permissible, or required. There is always a continuum between the complete "leave it to nature" solution, and the complete management based on active intervention to achieve a specified objective. Here there is the classic divide between the idealists and the realists. The idealists would leave things to nature, accepting a long time scale, and being happy with the result whatever it is. The realists tend to see the need for large-scale intervention to recreate landforms and water balances, and reintroduce the required vegetation and fauna. In this they tend to acknowledge that many reserves and nature areas are small and close to human habitation; nature areas in these situations have to achieve their objectives rapidly, otherwise they lose the public support and funding; and have to achieve a socially acceptable objective, which may be more

---

[1]   It would for example be unreasonable to expect the Dutch to return The Netherlands to a "natural" state by flooding and abandoning a large proportion of their country to the sea.

park-like than truly natural conditions. The "leave it to nature" programme is more often applicable to large wilderness areas.

Many small reserves (ponds, wetlands, small parks) are common and often close to urban areas. They are increasingly being managed, for example by wildlife groups or local councils, in pursuit of biodiversity action plans, local amenity plans, and in response to local residents' pressure. They perhaps demonstrate the whole range of possible ethical positions:

- Those who do not care about the environment have probably used the area as a dumping ground for many years.

- Many of the local residents subscribe as a minimum to a hedonistic principle – they find the idea pleasurable, but this normally imposes constraints on the management of the reserves: they must not appear unpleasant or unkempt (and so do not adversely affect property values); and management must not remove the amenity from their enjoyment for long periods.

- The utilitarian viewpoint would probably be indifferent to such developments, as it creates no immediate utility, and perhaps opposed to it if it diminishes the usefulness of the land. Such loss of utility might be countered by increases in adjacent property values.

- Consequentialists, particularly those subscribing to the stewardship argument, would almost certainly support such actions, on the grounds that it acts to preserve part of the landscape for future generations, provided that it was not part of greater development plans that they would otherwise oppose. (They are wary lest one a small reserve is tokenism.)

- Those who consider the environment as being intrinsically valuable would be less certain. Mostly, they would probably consider such small actions as irrelevant tokenism when compared to the need for a complete change of the mind-set of urban civilisation. Such reserves would almost certainly be heavily managed, and as such do not really meet the needs and rights of natural species.

- The extrinsic believers would also be less sure about the value, but would mainly support such reserves as a way of building support and understanding for the needs of the environment.

Here, as in so many examples, a whole variety of ethical attitudes and reactions are possible in response to what seems a simple action. Perhaps the great division is, as always, between the pragmatists and the idealists. Pragmatists see the advantage of working for small benefits, and so building towards a more environmentally friendly society. Idealists see it as a distraction from the real task that is to fundamentally change society.

Care of wild animals

A related issue that has recently come to prominence in some areas is that of the care of wild animals, particularly those introduced into an area by human action. To what extent should human beings intervene in the care of wild animals? Most human beings, when confronted with a sick or distressed animal, generally respond with sympathy. It seems to be a natural reaction to want to offer some sort of care to animals, particularly the higher mammals with whom we can relate quite easily. When those animals are wild, the appropriateness of such action is questionable, and the reply can easily be, surely wild animals should be left to natural processes, which includes sickness and death. An example of the problems that arise in a specific situation is reported by Klaver *et al.* (2002). In The Netherlands large herbivores were introduced into wildlife parks to maintain the vegetation. Regular grazing of the vegetation in the parks is necessary to maintain an acceptable balance between open grassland and forest. The alternative to herbivores is one of manual intervention—mowing and forest clearance, which was considered unacceptable for a "wildlife" area. The animals, Heck oxen and Konik horses, were as close to a "wild" species as could be identified at the time, as the natural herbivores in the area had long been either extinct or domesticated. In technical terms, the arrangement worked well, but there were significant public outcries when, in winter, the animals appeared to be in poor state, even starving and diseased. The issue that was debated was: how wild were these animals, and what responsibility did the human managers have to these animals?

Here again, the reactions of the various parties can be identified and shown to differ according to their ethical viewpoint.

- The hedonistic attitude would almost certainly opt for full care and management of the wild animals. If the aim were to enjoy the sight of those animals, then the pleasurable requirement is that these animals appear well looked after and healthy. They would require a humane culling programme, so that the old and diseased were removed, and the numbers controlled to that level best suited to maintaining the most pleasing visual balance of the vegetation.

- Utilitarians would not necessarily care about the state of the animals. To them the issue would be the best (perhaps meaning cheapest) way of maintaining animal numbers at a level that best managed the vegetation. Like the hedonists they would probably support humane culling as the option least likely to lead to costly health interventions.

- The Consequentialists would have more difficulty. They would on the one hand see that the fate and welfare of the animals was the responsibility of those who put them there in the first place. They would also see the processes of disease and death of animals as part of the natural processes that they were attempting to foster. They would further wish to see the continued use of animals to achieve a "natural" vegetation control system without undue human interference. The notion of stewardship thus presents a paradox that cannot easily be resolved, and which was the subject of much of the subsequent debate.

- The supporters of intrinsic animal rights had less difficulty. To them the natural processes leading to death are as much part of the nature of the animals as their life. As such, they are clearly against intervention, and so would leave the ecosystem to achieve its own balance. To them human dislike of seeing diseased or dying animals is an opportunity for education, not intervention.

- The extrinsic supporters would tend to follow the intrinsic, particularly those who from a religious viewpoint

have a more positive view of death. They are also motivated by an attitude of care for animals, and so would
support culling to prevent suffering.

Thus the various ethical stances are again not united. In the
end, the debate concluded that animals were of differing
degrees of "wildness", and those on the edges of the reserve
were semi-wild, semi-domesticated. A compromise was
adopted in which limited human intervention was possible
for those animals presenting in a distressed situation at the
edges of the reserve, but those in the centre would be
unmanaged.

A parallel case, also from The Netherlands, was discussed by Bovenkerk *et al.* (2003), who examined the issues
associated with the sheltering of seals in the Waddensea.
Again the issues were to what extent was it ethically acceptable to take animals out of the wild, if even for short periods,
and if it was acceptable, was there then a duty to do so.
Bovenkerk and her colleagues found a variation in ethical
stances between the those working directly in the field
(park managers and shelter workers) who were in favour of
intervention, and the policy makers, who being more
removed from the immediate situation, were much less
sure about the appropriateness of such action.[2] In the
Waddensea, there is no really wild territory, and hence their
respondents were able to talk of degrees of wildness, and so
identify the same continuum as identified by Klaver *et al,*
(2002). However, Bovenkerk *et al.* were able to offer four
basic principles that might help clarify specific situations:

- Beneficence, the underlying moral priority of care for
  animals in distress.

- Respect for wildness, which deserves priority, and can in
  some cases over-ride the beneficence requirement.

- The second chance condition, which grants animals that
  have been plainly unlucky a second chance to live their
  wild lives, through some relatively minor human intervention.

---

[2]　One such worker commented, rather tartly, "animals from the wild
should be protected against animal-hugging social workers".

- The distributive justice principle, in which it is incumbent on human beings to try to reverse consequence of their own actions, and so for example care for animals damaged by pollution or other human acts (such as boat damage to seals).

In applying these principles, they identify the importance of the circumstances of each individual encounter with an animal. In each encounter, it is thus necessary to evaluate the degree of distress and its source, the magnitude of the intervention required to correct it, the degree to which this will affect the wildness of the animal, and the potential impacts, if any, on the ecology of the area. To them, there were no simple answers applicable in all cases, but a range of actions dependent upon the circumstances.

The role of UK agriculture and the countryside

After the 2001 Foot and Mouth epidemic, a number of government and other reviews were undertaken, which together considered the future of British agriculture. (Among them: DETR, 2000; DETR, 2002, UK Cabinet Office, 2002; DEFRA, 2002, Food Ethics Council, 2001.) These reviews are important in showing that there was a developing consensus that the country as a whole was unsure about the direction of British agriculture. There was an underlying feeling that modern farming methods were destroying the countryside, polluting soil and water, and producing food of uncertain quality and purity. These perhaps focussed a general feeling that farming was no longer the environmentally friendly activity it was once perceived to be. (That the facts are more complex is perhaps less relevant than the perception, because perception is the force that drives government and public actions in the environment.)

In historical context, British agriculture has been heavily subsidised since 1945, following the experiences of the war years in which Britain had been shown to be vulnerable by relying on imported foodstuffs. However, in the 1970s, as European food surpluses became a fact of farming, a series of measures were brought into place to reduce production, and eventually came to replace agricultural subsidies with agri-environmental schemes (see Martin, 2000, for an historical summary). This was, in effect, the implementation of the "decoupling" component of the reform of the European Common Agricultural Policy, in which subsidies and support to rural and farming communities was separated from subsidies for agricultural production. At the same time, it became clear how much the largely urban tax-paying majority was paying the farming community by way of subsidies,[3] and that public started to consider that it ought to have a say in the future of farming. Within that context, there are thus several schools of thought that again reflect the varying discourse groups and ethical viewpoints.

Two critical groups are the farmers and the relevant government ministry (currently the Department for the Environment, Food and Rural Affairs, DEFRA). The majority of the government action comes from the problem-solving discourse group: they are either the bureaucrats that ask the experts, or the experts themselves, who see issues in agriculture as technical issues that need solving. Policy is often informed by a series of public consultations in which a technical proposal is put forwards, and comments invited. The DETR/Cabinet Office Consultation on "Farming and Food: a sustainable future" is one such example, (DETR, 2002; UK Cabinet Office, 2002), but there is a flow of such documents. These are still very much within the "ask the experts" sphere, although open to non-expert responses.

In ethical terms, most of the government actors fall within the utilitarian or stewardship categories. The utilitarian stance, particularly the reliance on cost benefit analysis for resolution of planning issues, is deeply embedded in legislation and it is the author's personal experience that the majority of government officials[4] are motivated by

---

[3]   The 2007 provisional gross statistics for agriculture, published by DEFRA on its web site, showed that from a gross output of £15,781 million; total farm income was £2,538 million, and subsidies £2,980 million. At the national scale, subsidies thus exceeded farm income.

[4]   A group within which the author worked for over 20 years. There is of course a wide variety of opinion within such a large body of people, and this is simply a sweeping generalisation based on personal experience.

consequentialist, mainly stewardship, considerations. There is a general wish to preserve and pass on the land to future generations, that extends first to a desire to preserve the land from destruction, secondly to enhance its natural value, and thirdly to actively promote environmental schemes.

Stewardship arguments probably also find a natural home with the farming community. It is a common theme for farmers to talk of passing on their land in "good heart" to the next generation, meaning with the soil fertility maintained, and the farming infrastructure in good repair. It is thus often with a heavy heart that many farmers move on from traditional practices to newer methods, involving more chemicals, larger scales of production, succumbing to the onward tread of progress in the production of cheap food. However, farmers are unable to survive economically unless they adopt modern methods, and adapt to modern markets. Within that broad spectrum of farmers, there are of course those who are motivated primarily by economic considerations. These are those who adopt a basically utilitarian stance, in which the land is seen primarily as their "factory floor" where they produce the optimum output of crops for a maximum profit. Equally, and for the environment, fortunately, there are those who want to manage their land in an environmentally friendly way. Such farmers are now helped by agri-environmental schemes, but many would adopt environmental management options in any case. These are frequently motivated by a love for the countryside and for the wild life within it. This might appear to be a degree of hedonism, but is probably more an implicit, unarticulated acknowledgement of the intrinsic value of nature.

The non-rural population creates two major pressures on agriculture, as consumers and tourists. As consumers we all eat food, and agriculture at its most basic is concerned with the production of that food. As consumers of farm products, the urban majority thus has a very direct influence on the fate of the small proportion that make their living from agriculture. Because of the immediate social impact of food prices, governments have been concerned to keep them low, and this policy has in the past been part of the rationale for farm subsidies. There is thus a consistent utilitarian economic thread, which concentrates on the availability of cheap food whilst maintaining farm incomes.

In the past 20 years or so, a speciality market has developed for "organic" food, produced in ways that are considered to be more environmentally friendly, and which is perceived to be in some way "better". Whatever one thinks of the organic movement, it is clear now that the market for such produce is fundamentally affecting how a proportion of the farmers operate. In some terms, this might be just pure hedonism on behalf of the consumers (they buy organic products because they prefer them), and opportunistic market response by the farmers (if they want to buy it, we will produce it). However, there is often underlying it an implicit stewardship argument in favour of organic methods which are thought of as more "natural".

The second big way in which the urban majority interact with the farming world is as consumers of the rural landscape (Barnett & Scruton, 1998). Some of them consume it quite directly, as they buy properties in rural areas. In doing so, they often try impose their own ideals of the countryside on their surrounds. Others "consume" the countryside by visiting it. In some areas, the tourist trade is as economically important as the income generated from farming itself, if not more so. In all of this consumption, the urban dwellers are often motivated as much by the myths and images of the countryside as by the actuality.

Again, the attitudes of those visiting or living in the countryside vary enormously, including perhaps all varieties of ethical opinion. To some, perhaps all, it must include an element of hedonism; they visit the countryside because they enjoy it, but many more adopt much more concerned attitudes towards the countryside, and the natural world. Many show this concern through membership of the voluntary bodies that work to preserve specific areas, or to manage reserves for birds or other ecosystems. The widespread membership of such bodies is a mark of the concern felt for wild areas, implying an underlying stewardship ethic.

There are thus a wide variety of attitudes and ethics underlying the visitors to the country landscape, and the farms that so often form it. Inevitably, these differing views can lead to conflicts, and rural life is full of (probably apocryphal) stories of conflicts between traditional farmers and newcomers; but these are not simply conflicts between those who must earn a living and those who want the mythical views of an idealised countryside. More often the conflicts arise because of different ethical views, between those who have a utilitarian ethic and those who want to affirm the intrinsic value of all components of the countryside. Additionally, there are those that would want to revolutionise the whole face of agriculture, as part of a reconstruction of western culture. A deep ecological viewpoint could perhaps require a cessation of much agriculture, and a return to naturalness for large areas of the world, that could only be achieved through a massive reduction in the world's human population.

Others with a religious viewpoint might wish to support the agricultural enterprise as part of the provision of a good creator for his creatures. This is certainly the main line Christian position, which affirms the goodness of God in providing for humankind, although at the same time requiring the even distribution of those good gifts. Other religions have an implicitly similar view if they also affirm the need to meet the needs of fellow humans. If our religion requires us to feed those who are hungry, we must have the means to do so.

The human population of the Earth

Almost any discussion of the environment at the whole Earth scale inevitably includes a discussion of the size of the world's human population. "In periods of population increase, environmentalists are sometimes tempted to treat population as the main source of environmental problems" (Attfield, 2003, p. 141). This is exemplified in the "Platform" of the Deep Ecology movement (Naess & Rothenberg, 1989) already quoted on page 78. Almost all of the issues associated with the degradation of the environment are related in some way to the size of the human population. The exponential growth of CO_2 in the atmosphere is paralleled by the growth of the human population, and the link is obvious. At the same time, the decline of many species is due to the expansion of human populations at the expense of wildlife habitats.

The current (2000) estimate of world population is 6 billion, potentially doubling by 2050 (Woolf, 2001). Discussions of population normally refer back to the exchange between Condoret and Malthus at the end of the eighteenth century. It is perhaps simplistic to view Condoret as an enlightened optimist, and Malthus as a gloomy misanthrope, but both saw the same issue, that continued increases in population numbers present a problem. The optimists hope that continued technological development and the accompanying increase in human well being leads to a decrease in fertility—hence the dictum that "development is the best contraceptive". Pessimists however observe that fertility rates are highest in the poorest areas of the world where high infant mortality rates, and lack of social provision for the elderly conspire to drive up the fertility rate. If development benefits are not cascaded to the poor, then it will do little to reduce the reproductive rate.

What these arguments make clear is that population levels and especially the fertility rates, are tied up inextricably with the state of society. Solution of population problems then cannot be separated from issues of global justice and poverty, and in particular the role and place of women in society.

In reviewing three essays in their anthology, Gruen & Jamieson (1994, pp. 307–8 *et seq.*) report three distinct attitudes. One is represented by biologists (Paul and Anne Ehrlich) who argue forcibly that we must control the world population at a level below its current high levels. A second, presented by Frances Moore Lappé and Rachel Schurman, identifies the critical role of women, and especially their low status in most societies, as the key underlying issue that must be solved before the population issue can be resolved. The third essay, by Julian Simon, argues that the issue should not be within the domain of public decision-making or policies at all, but is essentially a personal matter that can only be settled within families and within communities. So sensitive is the matter that Ehrlich and Ehrlich report that when the US National Academy of Sciences was producing a report for the then US President (George Bush Senior) on "global environmental change" they omitted any mention of population issues, on the grounds that any mention of it would result in the rejection of the entire report. Mentioning population was then, and still remains, a taboo subject among many administrations around the globe.[5]

Consequently, there are all sorts of ethical issues associated with the control of the Earth's population. Assuming we can achieve control of the population in an ethically acceptable way, and that we can identify an acceptable target population size,[6] it is still by no means clear how a just or acceptable population control programme could be achieved. It is quite acceptable for individuals to want to restrict the own reproduction, and indeed to attempt to persuade others to follow suit: but an attempt to enforce population limits will require the action of some sort of authority, and in some sense a reduction of individual's rights. This could be perhaps established in a version of the Social Contract, in which individuals subsume their own rights for the good of Society. Otherwise, this is perhaps one of those situations where Clark's (1993) analysis applies: that only a religious ethic would justify the necessary personal sacrifices. Equally, if we use a straight utilitarian calculation, we inevitably end up with the rather counter-intuitive result that when we sum all the good over the whole population, we

---

[5]   An attitude not unaffected by the Vatican's opposition to the implementation of birth control measures.

[6]   Naess & Rothenberg (1989, pp. 140–1) quote a UN study which suggests that the carrying capacity of the Earth to sustain the population at the current level of the USA is 500 million; but then go on to suggest themselves that a figure of 100 million would be more acceptable.

could end up with less good if the population is much smaller, even if the good per unit population is higher. We can also come to the same sort of conclusion when we think of our stewardship with a responsibility to the future generations: how do we justify to them a reduction in their numbers? And will they be grateful? We can of course only act as our consciences dictate, as they cannot actually hold that discussion with ourselves. After all, planning for the future is a basic human trait, and is particularly relevant to problems as large as the Earth's population that will require several (perhaps many) generations to be resolved.

Consequently, the population issue remains one of the great taboos in green ethics and politics. Most environmental scientists see the point of the argument, but most do not want to be drawn into a lengthy, heated, and emotional debate. Governments and their administrations are even less keen to become involved, for the same reasons. Nevertheless, the taboo must be broken, if some sort of progress is to be made.

Climate change

It would be perverse to finish this book without in some way mentioning the biggest environmental issue facing the human race: that of climate change. This is after all where we started, with the quotation from Al Gore's film on the subject. There are perhaps three issues that need to be mentioned at the start.

First, there is little doubt of the facts of climate change. They have been presented many times, and with increasing authority and urgency (IPCC, 2007). Increasing human use of fossil fuels has dramatically increased the atmospheric content of carbon dioxide, with a resultant increase in global mean temperature. The projections are for an increase in the range of 3 to 5°C by the end of this century. There are of course many variants of this prediction, but the general pattern of an order of this magnitude is clear (IPCC, 2007 and the supporting reports).

Second, there is also little doubt that the impacts of this increase in temperature will be enormous, on both the human world and the natural world. Again, this has been the subject of many studies (e.g. IPCC, 2007). There is no need to enumerate them all, but to note that they represent an unprecedented shift in the global climate that means that there is no true wilderness, unaffected by human action, anywhere on the planet.

Thirdly, the scientific studies of the phenomenon have also shown what needs to be done about it: to reduce the quantity of CO_2 and other greenhouse gases in the atmosphere. This can only be achieved by a massive reduction in emissions, with perhaps a small contribution from carbon sequestration technology. The simple fact is that the human race has to change its behaviour away from fossil carbon-based energy systems.

These, baldly, are the facts of the matter. They are well known that it is impossible to say, "we don't know the facts—so we have no duty to act." The "inconvenient truth"[7] is that humanity has "soiled its own nest" so badly that it now must do something about it. The issue of why we should do so is again the subject of ethics, and thus of this book (see also Spencer & White, 2007). We can identify a number of immediate ethical ways on which we can argue for action on this issue.

1. The simple utilitarian argument is that impacts of climate change are going to be catastrophic for some people and some locations, and potentially unpleasant for most of the rest of us. As a species we need to put things right in order to reduce these consequences.

2. The consequentialist argument is that we are responsible for our actions. The issue of climate change is one for which we are all responsible. We all consume energy, mostly profligately. The current state of the planet is the result of the cumulative actions of multiple individuals. As individuals we cannot deny our actions are in

---

[7] The title of the Al Gore film we have already quoted.

some small part of the problem. Equally, we cannot ignore the fact the solution requires each individual to take their small part in putting right what has gone wrong, by reducing their own "carbon footprint". A phenomenon that is the result of the cumulative action of multiple individuals can only be corrected by a corresponding action by all individuals. We cannot leave it to others to sort out the mess.

3. We have also failed in our stewardship to the future. The Earth that we will pass on to our grandchildren will be a very different place from the world we ourselves inherited. In some ways it will be a better world — we must never loose sight of the gains of modern living, particularly modern medicine. But we find a world increasingly polluted, and with its natural life increasingly under threat. It is an open question whether our great-great grandchildren will be able to enjoy the sights of the wild animals that are such a source of fascination to our present age.

4. We have also failed in our stewardship towards the planet and its inhabitants themselves. However we allocate value to the wild and the natural, it is clear that this value has diminished over the past century. We have a duty towards whoever or whatever it is that we hold the position of stewardship, to put this right.

To sum up, whichever way we look at the problem of climate change, we have an ethical duty to do something about it, and that duty devolves to each one of us, to act both as individuals and as societies and nations and on a global scale.

It would be naïve to think that the resolution of the climate change problem is the only global issue facing humankind. Indeed, there are other global issues, notable among them the poverty and deprivation of the so-called Third World, which are equally urgent and undeniable. Consequently, the issue of global social justice is also an ethical priority that to an extent competes with, and also complements the climate change issue. Consequently, the two are often presented in parallel (as in Spencer & White, 2007). The inter-relationship between the two are explored by Adger *et al.* (2006), who argue that there is a clear need for "Fairness in adaptation to climate change". Some feel that "fairness" is too weak a concept to support the major actions required to underpin the measures necessary to achieve justice on a global scale. Again we come back to Clark's (1993) argument that only a religious, or quasi-religious view will generate both the commitment and the willingness to forgo personal benefit sufficient to change the climate. Governments are doing their best, based on hard economic arguments, but this is barely enough, and needs to be supported by a committed population.

Chapter 7

A personal statement

The reader who has managed to get this far might reasonably ask, where does the author himself stand on these issues? I am thus offering the following brief statement as an example of how one person reacts to all these issues. I do not expect you to follow my stance, but I feel I owe this much to the reader. You can of course skip it and close the book right now!

My personal stance is that we must care for the environment because it is good in its own right, that good coming from its relation with a creator God. That puts me within the Franciscan strand of Christianity that could sing of Brother Sun, and Sister Moon. The two essential revelations that I use to underpin this orientation are first that God is the creator, mover and sustainer of all that is, including the created order; and second that in the person of Jesus of Nazareth, God became a human being, and this shows a close affinity between creator and created.

This is of course never the whole of the story, because I also find the environment beautiful and fascinating, as well as vulnerable and damaged. My career as an environmental scientist has been motivated first by a fascination with the natural, world, and secondly with the need to develop the techniques for controlling human management of it. I want to rectify the damage, and so preserve the beauty and the joy of creation for all who follow my generation, which is why I dedicate this book to my grandchildren.

The result is that I see the need for a radical shift in the nature of Western civilisation, but would wish to achieve this by progressive change, not by revolution. I can thus see a number of fundamental issues that need resolving:

1. We need to come to terms with the need for some sort of population planning. The current exponential increase in the human population cannot be sustained indefinitely, and I personally would be happier seeing the population stabilized significantly below current levels.

2. We have to create low carbon industrial and life style profiles. There are many options for the doing of this, including the continued development of technology, and the wide adoption of non-renewable energy production systems.[1]

3. We need to restructure the world economy so it does not need to expand all the time. We thus need to work towards systems that focus on longevity of goods, with a repair and mend mentality replacing the disposable and replacement mentality of today.[2] It also needs to be continuously developing towards the use of renewable rather than non-renewable resources.

4. At the same time, we need to address the issues of global poverty and deprivation, and in particular the need to increase the quality of life for the Third World.

5. Social justice must always be addressed in parallel with those of the environment. Among these issues is the role of women in many economies and societies.

6. We need to curb our need to be always travelling. Travelling itself is neither inherently good or bad, but the consequences in terms of carbon footprint and the despoliation of the countryside by roads,

[1] Although this is not a central issue, I have no inherent objection to the adoption of nuclear energy, provided sufficient care is taken and the waste disposed of sensibly. This viewpoint is indeed far from universal among environmentalists, many of whom are opposed to nuclear fuels.

[2] The obsession with fashion and the fashionable thus needs to be restrained.

railways and airports, needs to be reduced. Some of this can be addressed by technology, with for example the increasing use of telecommunications removing the need for many movements.

This wish list is of course idealistic, but perhaps no worse for being just that. It gives me, and perhaps others, a goal to work towards. It requires a change in the mindset of modern civilisation that is almost revolutionary, but would aim to see it, and its results, implemented by steady progress and change, in which developing technology will have a part (but only a part) to play. In this I am not anti-technology, but require technology to be at the service of humanity, and so appropriately configured.

This programme is initially optimistic, because I believe that humanity, aided by the inspiration of the Holy Spirit, has in the past risen to its challenges. It is also realistic, in that I assume it will take a long time to implement. Perhaps if it has taken over 250 hundred years from the start of the industrial era to get the planet into the mess it is now, then a reasonable estimate might be that it will take up to 500 years to put it right. Environmental reform has to adopt a lengthy time framework, which is why we pass on the concern to our children and grandchildren, so that they may continue the work begun at the start of this millennium.

Chapter 8

Conclusions

It seems that there are many possible answers to the question: why care for the Earth? This review has tried to demonstrate the breadth of opinion that can be identified in environmental ethics. These range from the simple answer: because we like it, to the more complex arguments that see the environment that is something of value in itself, that we must protect from the effects of human actions.

Initially it might seem that all these differing viewpoints might lead to confusion. Can there even be such a thing as a Green Movement, if it is underlain by so many differing viewpoints? The answer has to be yes — simply because we see it and observe it. But when we try to engage or debate with the movement we find many different strands within it. In order for that debate to be successful, we need to know where our fellow debaters stand on all sorts of issues. I hope that by identifying some of the threads, I will have illuminated the ethical position of some of the participants in the environmental debate. By understanding our fellow debaters, we can then engage in full dialogue, rather than shouting slogans at each other. That surely is a starting point for progress.

Despite all we have said, there are those who still do not care for the environment. We can perhaps understand that response from dwellers in modern cities who isolate themselves from the natural world, or from those whose life circumstances constrain their horizons to the issues of sheer survival. Those of us who care for the environment therefore need to work to expand those horizons, so that all humanity can share the same love for the environment, and share the same joys. Perhaps only by doing this, as well as engaging with the specifically environmental issues, will we be able to hand the environment over to our grand-children — not because we care for it, but because we have taught their generation to care for it after us.

Future generations may forgive us if, trying to care for the Earth, we get it wrong; but they certainly will not forgive us if we see the problems, and do not care about the conse-quences. It is up to us to make sure that we pass the world on to future generations, in as good a state as we can possibly do so. Future generations will look back the start of the twenty-first century as the point where the threefold prob-lems of population, climate change, and social justice have all come to a crisis point. They will judge us on our willing-ness to try to resolve the problems.

References

Adams, W.M., (2003) *Future Nature: A vision for conservation.* (2nd revised edition) London: Earthscan, 276 pp.

Adger, W.N., Paavola, J., Huq, S. & Mace, M.J., editors (2006) Fairness in adaptation to climate change. Cambridge Massachusetts: The MIT Press, 319 pp.

Almond, Brenda (1991) Rights. In Peter Singer, editor, *A Companion to Ethics,* Oxford: Blackwell, p. 259-269.

Armstrong A.C. & Bradley, C. (2007) Resolution of conflict in wetland management: The Somerset Levels, UK. In *Wetlands: Monitoring, Modelling and Management.* Ed. T.Okruszko, E.Maltby, J.Szatylowicz, D.Swiatek & W.Kotowski. London: Taylor & Francis, p. 331-338.

Armstrong, A.C (2000) Ethical issues in nature protection. *Physics and Chemistry of the Earth, Part B: Hydrology, Oceans And Atmosphere,* **25:** 641-644.

Armstrong, A.C. (2006) Ethical Issues in water use and sustainability. *Area:* **38:** 9-15.

Armstrong, A.C. (2007) Towards a water ethic. In: *Managing Water Resources in a Changing Physical and Social Environment.* Ed. P.J.Robinson, T.Jones & M-k. Woo. Rome: Societa Geografica Italiana, p. 7-15.

Armstrong, A.C., Caldow, R., Hodge, I. D. and Treweek, J. (1995) Restoring wetlands: the hydrological, ecological and socio-economic dimensions. In: J.Hughes & L.Heathwaite. (eds.) *Hydrology and Hydrochemistry of British wetlands.* Chichester: J.Wiley & Sons, p. 445-466.

Attenborough, David. (1979) *Life on Earth:: A Natural History.* London: Collins, 319 pp.

Attfield, Robin (1991) *The Ethics of Environmental Concern.* (Second edition). Athens, Georgia: University of Georgia Press, 249 pp.

Attfield, Robin (2001) Christianity. In: Jamieson, D., editor (2001) *A Companion to Environmental Philosophy* Oxford: Blackwell's Companions to Philosophy Series, Blackwell, p.96-110.

Attfield, Robin (2003) *Environmental Ethics,* Cambridge: Polity Press, 232pp.

Barnes, J., editor (1995) *The Cambridge Companion to Aristotle.* Cambridge: Cambridge University Press, 404 pp.

Barnett, A. & Scruton, R. (1998) *Town and Country*. London: Jonathon Cape, 379 pp.

Barton, John (1999) *Ethics and the Old Testament*. London: SCM Press, 100pp.

Batchelor, M. & Brown, K., editors (1992) *Buddhism and Ecology*. London: Cassell, World Wide Fund for Nature, World religions and Ecology series, 114 pp.

Beck, U. (1992) *Risk Society: Towards a new modernity*. (Translation by M.Ritter). London: Sage Publications, 260 pp.

Blatz, C.V., (1994) Coming full circle: ethical Issues in traditional and industrialized agriculture. In: American Society of Agronomy, *Agricultural Ethics: Issues for the 21st century* ASA Special Publication 57, p.33-42.

Bonting, S.L., (2005) *Creation and Double Chaos: Science and Theology in discussion*. Minneapolis: Fortress Press, 275 pp.

Botzler, R.G. & Armstrong, S.J. (1998) *Environmental Ethics: Divergence and convergence*. 2nd edition. Boston: McGraw Hill, 600 pp.

Bovenkerk, B., Stafleu, F., Tramper, R., Vorstenbosch, J., & Brom, W.A. (2003) To act or not to act? Sheltering animals from the wild: a pluralistic account of a conflict between animal and environmental ethics. *Ethics, Place and Environment*, **6**: 13-26.

Breuilly, E. & Palmer, M., editors (1992) *Christianity and Ecology*. London: Cassell, World Wide Fund for Nature, World religions and Ecology series, 118 pp.

Brennan, Andrew (2001) Nineteenth- and twentieth-century philosophy. In: Jamieson, D., editor (2001) *A Companion to Environmental Philosophy* Oxford: Blackwell's Companions to Philosophy Series, Blackwell, p.146-160.

Brooke, J. & Cantor, G. (1998) *Reconstructing Nature: The engagement of science and religion*. Edinburgh: T&T Clark, 367 pp.

Bryant, Barbara (1996) *Twyford Down – roads, campaigning and environmental law*. London: E & FN Spon, 334 pp.

Callicott, J. Baird (1989) *In Defense of the Land Ethic*. Albany: State University of New York Press, 325 pp.

Callicott, J. Baird (1999) *Beyond the Land Ethic*. Albany: State University of New York Press, 427 pp.

Callicott, J. Baird (2001) The Land Ethic. In: Jamieson, D., editor (2001) *A Companion to Environmental Philosophy* Oxford: Blackwell's Companions to Philosophy Series, Blackwell, p.204-217.

Carnap, R. (1966) *An introduction to the Philosophy of Science* (edited by Martin Gardner), New York: Basic Books, 300 pp.

Carone, G.R. (2001) The classical Greek Tradition. In: Jamieson, D., editor (2001) *A Companion to Environmental Philosophy* Oxford: Blackwell's Companions to Philosophy Series, Blackwell, p.67-80.

Carson, Rachel (1962) *Silent Spring*. Reprinted with an afterword by Linda Lear, 1999, London: Penguin, 323 pp.

Clark, J., Burgess, J. & Harrison, C.M. (2000) "I struggled with this money business": respondents' perspectives on contingent valuation. *Ecological Economics* **33:** 45-62.

Clark, Stephen R L (1993) *How to Think about the Earth: Philosophical and theological models for ecology.* London: Mowbray, 168 pp.

Connelly, J & Smith, G. (2003) *Politics and the Environment* (2nd edition). London & New York: Routledge, 390 pp.

Cronon, W., editor (1997) *John Muir: Nature Writings.* New York: The library of America, 888 pp.

Dawkins, R. (1976, 2nd edition 1989) *The Selfish Gene.* Oxford: Oxford University Press, 352 pp.

DEFRA, Department for Environment Food and Rural Affairs. (2005). *Environmental Stewardship: Look after your land and you will be rewarded.* London: DEFRA PF 10487, London, 16 pp.

DEFRA, Department for Environment, Food and Rural Affairs. (2002). *The Strategy for Sustainable Farming and Food: Facing the future.* London: DEFRA, 51 pp.

DETR, UK Department for the Environment, Transport and the Regions. (2000). *Our Countryside: The future.* London: Her Majesties Stationary Office, Cm4909, 176 pp.

DETR, UK Department for the Environment, Transport and the Regions. (2002). *Response to the report of the Policy Commission on the future of farming and food by HM government.* London: Her Majesties Stationary Office. Cm5709, 16 pp.

Dryzek, J. S., Downers, D., Hunold, C., Schlosberg, D. with Hernes, H-K. (2003) *Green States and Social Movements: Environmentalism in the United States, United Kingdom, Germany & Norway.* Oxford: Oxford University Press, 223 pp.

Dryzek, John S. (1997) *The Politics of the Earth: Environmental discourses.* Oxford: Oxford University Press, 220 pp.

Dwyer, J.C. & Hodge, I.D. (1996) *Countryside In Trust: Land management by conservation, recreation and amenity organisations.* Chichester: John Wiley & Sons, 299 pp.

Elliot, R. (1982) Faking Nature. *Inquiry* **25:** 81-93. Reprinted in Elliot, R. editor (1995) p.76-88.

Elliot, Robert, editor. (1995) *Environmental Ethics.* Oxford: Oxford Readings in Philosophy, Oxford University Press, 255 pp.

EU (2000) Directive 2000/60 of the European Parliament and of the Council of 23 October 2000 establishing a framework for community action in the field of water policy. Luxembourg.

Everitt, C., Ebenezer, C., Watts, D., Pennington, B., Jones, A. & Booth, M. (1985) *Part III The Christian Testament since the Bible.* London: Firethorn Press, 382 pp.

Evernden, N. (1992) *The Social Creation of Nature.* Baltimore: The Johns Hopkins University Press, 181 pp.

Food Ethics Council (2001) *After FMD: Aiming for a values-driven agriculture.* Southwell, Nottinghamshire: The Food Ethics Council, 40 pp.

Foster, J, (1997) Introduction: Environmental value and the scope of economics. In *Valuing Nature: Ethics, economics and the environment* ed. John Foster. London & New York: Routledge, p. 1-17.

Foster, S.E. (2002) Aristotle and the Environment. *Environmental Ethics* **24:** 409-428.

Gatward, G., (2001) *Livestock Ethics: Respect, and our duty of care for farm animals.* Lincoln: Chalcombe publications, 304 pp.

Gold, M., (1995) *Animal Rights: Extending the circle of compassion.* Oxford: Jon Carpenter, 153pp.

Green, C. (2000) If only life were that simple: Optimism and Pessimism in Economics. *Physics and Chemistry of the Earth (B)*, **25:** 205-212.

Grove-White, R. (1997) The environmental 'valuation controversy: observations on its recent history and significance. In *Valuing Nature: Ethics, economics and the environment* ed. John Foster. London & New York: Routledge, p. 21-31.

Gruen, Lori & Jamieson, Dale, editors (1994) *Reflecting on Nature: Readings in environmental Philosophy.* Oxford: Oxford University Press, 362 pp.

Haslam, Henry (2005) *The Moral Mind.* Exeter: Imprint Academic, 106 pp.

Hayter, Teresa (1971) *Aid as Imperialism.* Harmondsworth: Penguin, 222 pp.

Hobbes, Thomas. (1651) *Leviathan.* Available in many editions. For example with introduction by A.D.Lindsay, (1914) London: Dent, 398 pp.

Hooykaas, R. (1972) *Religion and the Rise of Modern Science.* Edinburgh: Scottish Academic Press, 162 pp.

Hughes, Ted. (1997) *Tales from Ovid.* London: Faber & Faber Ltd, 264 pp.

Innes, M.M. (1995) *The Metamorphoses of Ovid.* Harmondsworth: Penguin Books, 363 pp.

IPCC Intergovernmental Panel on Climate Change (2007). *Climate Change 2007: Synthesis Report.* Summary for Policy makers. 22p. See also the Reports of the three working groups: WGI: The Physical Science Basis, WGII: Impacts Adaptation and Vulnerability, and WG3III: Mitigation of Climate Change. All reports are published by Cambridge University Press or available from the IPCC web site.

Jamieson, D., editor (2001) *A Companion to Environmental Philosophy* Oxford: Blackwell's Companions to Philosophy Series, Blackwell, 531 pp.

Jordan, A., editor. (2002) *Environmental Policy in the European Union: Actors, Institutions and processes.* London: Earthscan publications, 354 pp.

Jorgensen, B.S., Wilson, M.A., & Heberlein, T.A. (2001) Fairness in the contingent valuation of environmental public goods: attitude toward paying for environmental improvements at two levels of scope. *Ecological Economics* **36:** 133-148.

Keller, C. (1993) Talk about the weather: The greening of eschatology. In Adams, C., editor *Ecofeminism and the Sacred*. New York: Continuum, pp. 30-49.

Khalid, F.M. & O'Brien, J., editors (1992) *Islam and Ecology*. London: Cassell, World Wide Fund for Nature, World religions and Ecology series, 111 pp.

Kirchner, J.W. (2002) The Gaia hypothesis: Fact, theory and wishful thinking. *Climatic Change.* **52:** 391-408.

Klauer, B. (2000) Ecosystem prices: activity analysis applied to ecosystems. *Ecological Economics* **2000:** 473-486.

Klaver, I., Keulartz, J., van den Belt, H. & Gremmen, B. (2002) Born to be Wild: A pluralistic ethics concerning introduced large herbivores in the Netherlands. *Environmental Ethics:* **24:** 3-21.

Leopold, Aldo (1949) *A Sand County Almanac and sketches here and there.* Oxford: Oxford University Press, 228 pp.

Light, A. & Rolston, III. Holmes, editors (2003) *Environmental Ethics: an anthology* Oxford: Blackwell, 554 pp.

Linzey, Andrew. (1994) *Animal Theology*. London: SCM Press, 214 pp.

Loomis, J., Kent, P., Strange, L., Fausch, K. & Covich, A. (2000) Measuring the total economic value of restoring ecosystem services in an impaired river basin: results from a contingent value survey. *Ecological Economics* **33:** 103-117.

Lovelock, J. (1979) *Gaia: A new look at life on Earth.* Oxford: Oxford University Press, 157 pp.

Lovelock, James. (1988) *The Ages of Gaia: a biography of the living Earth.* Oxford: Oxford University Press, 252 pp.

Lowdermilk, W.C. (1953) *Conquest of the Land Through Seven Thousand Years.* USDA Soil Conservation Service Bulletin 99, 30 pp.

Lowenthal, D., editor (1965) *Man and Nature by George Perkins Marsh,* edited from original published in 1864, and with an introduction. Cambridge Massachusetts: Belhaven Press, 472 pp.

MacQuarrie, J. (1983) Immanentism. In: A.Richardson & J.Bowden *A New Dictionary of Christian Theology,* London: SCM, pp.287.

MAFF, Ministry of Agriculture Fisheries and Food (1975) *Food from our own resources,* London: Her Majesties Stationary Office, Cmnd. 6020, 21 pp.

Martin, J, (2000) *The Development of Modern Agriculture: British farming since 1931.* Basingstoke: MacMillan Press, 236 pp.

Mathews, Freya. (1991) Value in Nature and Meaning in Life. Extract from Chapter 4 of *The Ecological Self,* London: Routledge, reprinted in Elliot (1995), p. 142-154.

McCormick, John. (1995) *The Global Environmental Movement.* 2nd edition. Chichester: John Wiley & Sons, 312 pp.

McFague, S. (1997) *Super, Natural Christians.* London: SCM, 207 pp.

Meadows, D.H., Meadows, D.L., Randers, J. & Behrens III, W.W. (1972) *The Limits To Growth: A report for the Club of Rome's project on the predicament of mankind.* London: Pan Books, 205 pp.

Midgley, Mary (1978) *Beast and Man: The roots of human nature.* (Revised edition 1995) London: Routledge, 365 pp.

Midgley, Mary (1983) Duties Concerning Islands. In: R. Elliot & A.Gare, eds. *Environmental Philosophy*, St. Lucia: University of Queensland Press, Reprinted in Elliot, R., editor (1995), p. 89-103.

Momaday, N. Scott (1998) A first American's view. In Botzler, R.G. & Armstrong, S.J. (1998) *Environmental Ethics: Divergence and convergence.* 2nd edition. Boston: McGraw Hill, p.252-256.

Moncrief, L.W. (1970) The cultural basis for our environmental crisis. *Science* **170:** 508-511.

Murphy, Charles M. (1989) *At Home on Earth: Foundations for a Catholic Ethic of the Environment.* New York: Crossroad, 180 pp.

Mythen, G. (2004) *Ulrich Beck: A critical introduction to the risk society.* London: Pluto Press, 216 pp.

Naess, A & Rothenberg, D. (1989) *Ecology, community and lifestyle.* Cambridge: Cambridge University Press, 223 pp.

Nussbaum, M.C. (1986) *The Fragility of Goodness: Luck and tragedy in Greek tragedy and philosophy.* Cambridge: Cambridge University Press, 544 pp.

O'Neil J. (2003) The Varieties of Intrinsic Value. In A.Light & Holmes Rolston III, editors, *Environmental Ethics: An anthology.* Oxford: Blackwell, p. 131-142.

Odum, E.P. (1966). *Ecology.* New York: Holt Rinehart & Winston, York, 152 pp.

Paine, Thomas (1791) *The Rights of Man.* See for example the edition edited by Eric Foner (1984), New York and London: Penguin Books, 281 pp.

Palmer, Clare (1992) Stewardship: a case study in environmental ethics. In *The Earth Beneath: A critical guide to green theology* ed. I. Ball, M.Goodall, C.Palmer & J.Reader. London: SPCK, p. 67-86.

Perman, D. (1973) *Cublington: A blueprint for resistance.* London: Bodley Head, 192 pp.

Popper, K R (1935) *Logik der Forschung.* English Translation: *The Logic of Scientific Discovery*, London: Hutchinson, 1959, and subsequent revisions.

Prime, Ranchor (1992) *Hinduism and Ecology: Seeds of truth.* London: Cassell, World Wide Fund for Nature, World religions and Ecology series, 118 pp.

Priscoli, J.D., Dooge, J. & Llamas, Ramon. (2004) *Water and Ethics: Overview.* UNESCO Series on Water and Ethics, Paper 1. Paris: UNESCO, 32 pp.

Purseglove, J. (1988) *Taming the Flood: A natural history of rivers and wetlands.* Oxford: Oxford University Press, 307 pp.

Radford Reuther, Rosemary (1992) *God and Gaia: An ecofeminist theology of Earth healing.* English edition London: SCM Press, 1993, 310 pp.

Radford Ruether, Rosemary (1996). *Women Healing Earth: Third world women on Ecology, Feminism, and Religion.* Maryknoll: Orbis Books.

Richards, M.W. & Tyabji, H. (2008) *Tigers*. London: New Holland Publishers, 160 pp.

Rolston III, Holmes (1988) *Environmental Ethics: Duties to and values in the Natural world*. Philadelphia: Temple University Press, 391 pp.

Rolston, H., III (1994) Value in Nature and Nature of Value, in R.Attfield & A.Belsey, editors, *Philosophy and Natural Environment*, Royal Institute of Philosophy Supplement. Cambridge: Cambridge University Press. Reprinted in Light & Rolston (2003), p.143-153.

Rose, A., editor (1992) *Judaism and Ecology* London: Cassell, World Wide Fund for Nature, World religions and Ecology series, 142 pp.

Routley, Richard & Routley, Val. (1979) Against the inevitability of Human Chauvinism. In: K. Goodpaster & K.Sayre, editors, *Ethics and Problems of the 21st Century*. Notre Dame, University of Notre Dame Press, Reprinted in Elliot, R., editor (1995), p. 104-128.

Russell, B. (1945) *A History of Western Philosophy*. New York: Simon & Schuster, 895 pp.

Scarpa, R., Chilton, S.M., Hutchinson, W.G. & Buongiorno, J. (2000) Valuing the recreational benefits from the creation of nature reserves in Irish forests. *Ecological Economics* **33**: 237-250.

Schumacher, E.E. (1974) *Small Is Beautiful: A study of economics as if people mattered*. London: Abacus, 255 pp.

Sherman, N., editor (1999) *Aristotle's Ethics: Critical Essays*. Lanham Maryland: Rowman & Littlefield, 331 pp.

Singer, P. (1995) *Animal Liberation*. 2nd edition, with a new preface. London: Pimlico, an imprint of Random House, 320 pp. (First edition dated 1975).

Singer, P., editor. (1991) *A Companion to Ethics*. Oxford: Blackwell, 565 pp.

Small, B. & Jollands, N. (2006) Technology and ecological economics: Promethean technology, Pandorean potential. *Ecological Economics*, **56**: 343-358.

Smith, Pamela (1997) *What are they saying about Environmental Ethics?* New York: Paulist Press, 122 pp.

Spencer, Nick & White, Robert (2007) *Christianity, Climate Change, and Sustainable Living*. London: SPCK, 245 pp.

Stevenson, L. (1974) *Seven Theories of Human Nature*. Oxford: Oxford University Press, 128 pp.

Sylvan, Richard (1973) Is there a need for a new environmental ethic? In *Philosophy and Science: Morality and Culture: Technology and Man*, Proceedings of the XVth World Congress of Philosophy, Varno, Bulgaria, Sofia, 1973. Reprinted in Light & Rolston (2003).

Taliaferro, C. (2001) Early modern philosophy. In Jamieson, D. editor. *A Companion to Environmental Philosophy*. Blackwell's Companions to Philosophy Series, Oxford: Blackwell, p. 130-145.

Tawney, R.H. (1926) *Religion and the Rise of Capitalism*. (Penguin edition, 1938, 334 pp. West Drayton).

Thoreau, Henry David (1854) *Walden, or Life in the Woods.* (My copy was published in the World Classics Series in 1906 by Oxford University Press, 299 pp.)

Toulmin, S. (1953) *The Philosophy of Science.* (1967 ed., London: Hutchinson, 160 pp.

Tredennick, H. & Waterfield, R. (1990) *Conversations of Socrates.* Harmondsworth: Penguin Classics, 366pp.

Tucker, M.E. & D.R.Williams (1997) *Buddhism and Ecology: The interconnection of Dharma and Deeds.* Cambridge, Mass.: Harvard University Press, 467 pp.

Turner, F. (1997) *John Muir: From Scotland to the Sierra.* Edinburgh: Cannongate Press, 417 pp.

Turner, R.K., Pearce, D. & Bateman, I. (1994) *Environmental Economics: An elementary introduction.* London: Pearson Education, 328 pp.

Tyme, John, (1978) *Motorways versus Democracy.* London: Macmillan, 166 pp.

UK Cabinet Office. (2002) *Farming and Food: A sustainable future.* London: Cabinet Office, 12 pp.

Van Dieren, W., editor (1995) *Taking Nature into Account: A report to the club of Rome.* New York: Copernicus, Springer-Verlag, 332 pp.

Weldon, J.E.C., translator (1987) *Aristotle: The Nichomachean Ethics.* Amherst New York: Prometheus Books, 358 pp.

West, M.L. (1998) *Introduction to Hesiod: Theogany and Works and Days.* Oxford: Oxford University Press, 79pp.

White, L. (1967) The historical roots of our ecological crisis. *Science,* **155:** 1203-7. (also reprinted for example in Gruen & Jamieson, 1994, pp 5-14).

Whitt, L.A., Roberts, M., Norman, W. & Grieves, W. (2001) Indigenous perspectives. In Jamieson, D. editor. *A Companion to Environmental Philosophy.* Oxford: Blackwell's Companions to Philosophy Series, Blackwell, p. 3-20.

Wolf, C .(2001) Population . Indigenous perspectives. In Jamieson, D. editor. *A Companion to Environmental Philosophy.* Oxford: Blackwell's Companions to Philosophy Series, Blackwell, p. 362-276.

World Commission on Environment and Development (1987) *Our Common Future.* Oxford: Oxford University Press.

Index

2008–2009

SOCIETAS

essays in political and cultural criticism
imprint-academic.com/societas

Who Holds the Moral High Ground?

Colin J Beckley and Elspeth Waters

Meta-ethical attempts to define concepts such as 'goodness', 'right and wrong', 'ought' and 'ought not', have proved largely futile, even over-ambitious. Morality, it is argued, should therefore be directed primarily at the reduction of suffering, principally because the latter is more easily recognisable and accords with an objective view and requirements of the human condition. All traditional and contemporary perspectives are without suitable criteria for evaluating moral dilemmas and without such guidance we face the potent threat of sliding to a destructive moral nihilism. This book presents a possible set of defining characteristics for the foundation of moral evaluations, taking into consideration that the female gender may be better disposed to ethical leadership.

128 pp., £8.95/$17.90, 9781845401030 (pbk.), January 2008, *Societas,* Vol.32

Froude Today

John Coleman

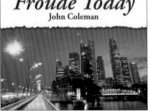

A.L. Rowse called fellow-historian James Anthony Froude the 'last great Victorian awaiting revival'. The question of power is the problem that perplexes every age: in his historical works Froude examined how it applied to the Tudor period, and defended Carlyle against the charge that he held the doctrine that 'Might is Right'.

Froude applied his analysis of power to the political classes of his own time and that is why his writings are just as relevant today. The historian and the prophet look into the inner meaning of events – and that is precisely what Froude did – and so are able to make judgments which apply to ages far beyond their own. The last chapters imagine what Froude would have said had he been here today.

96 pp., £8.95/$17.90, 9781845401047 (pbk.), March 2008, *Societas,* Vol.33

The Enemies of Progress

Austin Williams

This polemical book examines the concept of sustainability and presents a critical exploration of its all-pervasive influence on society, arguing that sustainability, manifested in several guises, represents a pernicious and corrosive doctrine that has survived primarily because there seems to be no alternative to its canon: in effect, its bi-partisan appeal has depressed critical engagement and neutered politics.

It is a malign philosophy of misanthropy, low aspirations and restraint. This book argues for a destruction of the mantra of sustainability, removing its unthinking status as orthodoxy, and for the reinstatement of the notions of development, progress, experimentation and ambition in its place.

Al Gore insists that the 'debate is over'. Here the auhtor retorts that it is imperative to argue against the moralizing of politics.

Austin Williams tutors at the Royal College of Art and Bartlett School of Architecture.

96 pp., £8.95/$17.90, 9781845400989 (pbk.), May 2008, *Societas,* Vol.34

Forgiveness: How Religion Endangers Morality

R.A. Sharpe

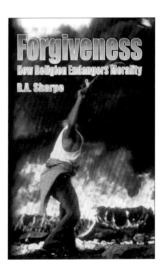

In his book *The Moral Case against Religious Belief* (1997), the author argued that some important virtues cease to be virtues at all when set in a religious context, and that, consequently, a religious life is, in many respects, not a good life to lead. In this sequel, his tone is less generous to believers than hitherto, because 'the intervening decade has brought home to us the terrible results of religious conviction'.

R.A. Sharpe was Professor Emeritus at St David's College, Lampeter. The manuscript of *Forgiveness* was prepared for publication by his widow, the philosopher Lynne Sharpe.

128 pp., £8.95 / $17.90, 9781845400835 (pbk.), July 2008, (*Societas* edition), Vol.35

To qualify for the reduced (subscription) price of £5/$10 for current and future volumes (£2.50/$5.00 for back volumes), please use the enclosed direct debit form or order via imprint-academic.com/societas

Healing, Hype or Harm? Scientists Investigate Complementary or Alternative Medicine

Edzard Ernst (ed.)

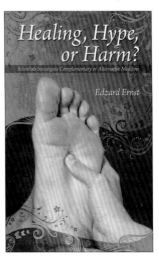

The scientists writing this book are not 'against' complementary or alternative medicine (CAM), but they are very much 'for' evidence-based medicine and single standards. They aim to counter-balance the many uncritical books on CAM and to stimulate intelligent, well-informed public debate.

TOPICS INCLUDE: What is CAM? Why is it so popular? Patient choice; Reclaiming compassion; Teaching CAM at university; Research on CAM; CAM in court; Ethics and CAM; Politics and CAM; Homeopathy in context; Concepts of holism in medicine; Placebo, deceit and CAM; Healing but not curing; CAM and the media.

Edzard Ernst is Professor of Complementary Medicine, Universities of Exeter and Plymouth.

190 pp., £8.95/$17.90, 9781845401184 (pbk.), Sept. 2008, *Societas,* Vol.36

The Balancing Act: National Identity and Sovereignty for Britain in Europe

Atsuko Ichijo

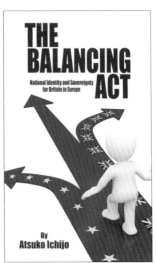

This is a careful examination of the historical formation of Britain and of key moments in its relations with the European powers. The author looks at the governing discourses of politicians, the mass media, and the British people.

The rhetoric of sovereignty among political elites and the population at large is found to conceive of Britain's engagement with Europe as a zero-sum game. A second theme is the power of geographical images – island Britain – in feeding the idea of the British nation as by nature separate and autonomous. It follows that the EU is seen as 'other' and involvement in European decision-making tends to be viewed in terms of threat. This is naive, as nation-states are not autonomous, economically, militarily or politically. Only pooling sovereignty can maximize their national interests.

Atsuko Ichijo is Senior Researcher in European Studies at Kingston University.

150 pp., £8.95/$17.90, 9781845401153 (pbk.), Nov. 2008, *Societas,* Vol.37

Seeking Meaning and Making Sense

John Haldane

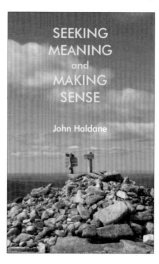

Here is an engaging collection of short essays that range across philosophy, politics, general culture, morality, science, religion and art.

The author contributes regularly to *The Scotsman* and a number of radio programmes. Many of these essays began life in this way, and retain their direct fresh style.

The focus is on questions of Meaning, Value and Understanding. Topics include: Making sense of religion, Making sense of society, Making sense of evil, Making sense of art and science, Making sense of nature.

John Haldane is Professor of Philosophy and Director of the Centre for Ethics, Philosophy and Public Affairs in the University of St Andrews.

128 pp., £8.95/$17.90, 9781845401221 (pbk.), Jan. 2009, *Societas,* Vol.38

Independent: The Rise of the Non-aligned Politician

Richard Berry

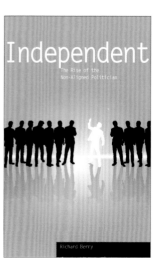

Martin Bell, Ken Livingstone and Richard Taylor (the doctor who became an MP to save his local hospital) are the best known of a growing band of British politicians making their mark outside the traditional party system.

Some (like Livingstone) have emerged from within the old political system that let them down, others (Bell, Taylor) have come into politics from outside in response to a crisis of some kind, often in defence of a perceived threat to their local town or district.

Richard Berry traces this development by case studies and interviews to test the theory that these are not isolated cases, but part of a permanent trend in British politics, a shift away from the party system in favour of independent non-aligned representatives of the people.

Richard Berry is a political and policy researcher and writer.

128 pp., £8.95/$17.90, 9781845401283 (pbk.), March 2009, *Societas,* Vol.39

Progressive Secular Society and other essays relevant to secularism

Tom Rubens

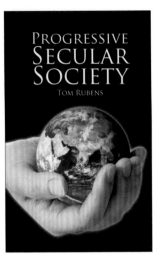

A progressive secular society is one committed to the widening of scientific knowledge and humane feeling. It regards humanity as part of physical nature and opposes any appeal to supernatural agencies or explanations. In particular, human moral perspectives are human creations and the only basis for ethics.

Secular values need re-affirming in the face of the resurgence of aggressive supernatural religious doctrines and practices. This book gives a set of 'secular thoughts for the day' – many only a page or two long – on topics as varied as Shakespeare and Comte, economics, science and social action.

Tom Rubens teaches in the humanities at secondary and tertiary levels.

128 pp., £8.95/$17.90, 9781845401320 (pbk.), May 2009, *Societas,* Vol.40

Self and Society (enlarged second edition)

William Irwin Thompson

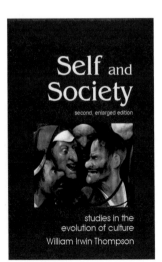

The book contains a series of essays on the evolution of culture, dealing with topics including the city and consciousness, evolution of the afterlife, literary and mathematical archetypes, machine consciousness and the implications of 9/11 and the invasion of Iraq for the development of planetary culture.

This enlarged edition contains an additional new second part, added to include chapters on 'Natural Drift and the Evolution of Culture' and 'The Transition from Nation-State to Noetic Polity' as well as two shorter reflective pieces.

The author is a poet, cultural historian and founder of the Lindisfarne Association. His many books include *Coming into Being: Artifacts and Texts in the Evolution of Consciousness.*

150 pp., £8.95/$17.90, 9781845401337 (pbk.), July 2009, *Societas,* Vol.41

Universities: The Recovery of an Idea (revised second edition)

Gordon Graham

RAE, teaching quality assessment, student course evaluation, modularization – these are all names of innovations in modern British universities. How far do they constitute a significant departure from traditional academic concerns? Using themes from J.H.Newman's *The Idea of a University* as a starting point, this book aims to address these questions.

'It is extraordinary how much Graham has managed to say (and so well) in a short book.' **Alasdair MacIntyre**

£8.95/$17.90, 9781845401276 (pbk), *Societas* V.1

God in Us: A Case for Christian Humanism

Anthony Freeman

God In Us is a radical representation of the Christian faith for the 21st century. Following the example of the Old Testament prophets and the first-century Christians it overturns received ideas about God. God is not an invisible person 'out there' somewhere, but lives in the human heart and mind as 'the sum of all our values and ideals' guiding and inspiring our lives.

The Revd. Anthony Freeman was dismissed from his parish for publishing this book, but remains a priest in the Church of England.

'Brilliantly lucid.' *Philosophy Now*
'A brave and very well-written book' *The Freethinker*

£8.95/$17.90, 9780907845171 (pbk), *Societas* V.2

The Case Against the Democratic State

Gordon Graham

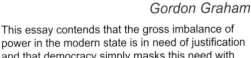

This essay contends that the gross imbalance of power in the modern state is in need of justification and that democracy simply masks this need with the illusion of popular sovereignty. The book points out the emptiness of slogans like 'power to the people', as individual votes do not affect the outcome of elections, but concludes that democracy can contribute to civic education.

'Challenges the reigning orthodoxy'. *Mises Review*

'Political philosophy in the best analytic tradition… scholarly, clear, and it does not require a professional philosopher to understand it' *Philosophy Now*

'An excellent candidate for inclusion on an undergraduate syllabus.' *Independent Review*

£8.95/$17.90, 9780907845386 (pbk), *Societas* V.3

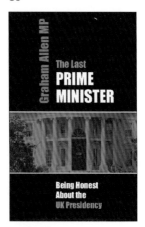

The Last Prime Minister
Graham Allen MP

This book shows how Britain has acquired an executive presidency by stealth. It is the first ever attempt to codify the Prime Minister's powers, many hidden in the mysteries of the royal prerogative. This timely second edition takes in new issues, including Parliament's impotence over Iraq.

> 'Iconoclastic, stimulating and well-argued.' **Vernon Bogdanor**, *Times Higher Education Supplement*

> 'Well-informed and truly alarming.' **Peter Hennessy**

> 'Should be read by anybody interested in the constitution.' **Anthony King**

£8.95/$17.90, 9780907845416 (pbk), *Societas* V.4

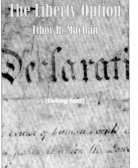

The Liberty Option
Tibor R. Machan

The Liberty Option advances the idea that it is the society organised on classical liberal principles that serves justice best, leads to prosperity and encourages the greatest measure of individual virtue. The book contrasts this Lockean ideal with the various statist alternatives, defends it against its communitarian critics and lays out some of its more significant policy implications. The author teaches ethics at Chapman University. His books on classical liberal theory include *Classical Individualism* (Routledge, 1998).

£8.95/$17.90, 9780907845638 (pbk), *Societas* V.5

Democracy, Fascism & the New World Order
Ivo Mosley

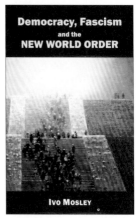

Growing up as the grandson of Sir Oswald, the 1930s blackshirt leader, made Ivo Mosley consider fascism with a deep and acutely personal interest. Whereas conventional wisdom sets up democracy and fascism as opposites, to ancient political theorists democracy had an innate tendency to lead to extreme populist government, and provided unscrupulous demagogues with the ideal opportunity to seize power. In *Democracy, Fascism and the New World Order* Mosley argues that totalitarian regimes may well be the logical outcome of unfettered mass democracy.

'Brings a passionate reasoning to the analysis'. *Daily Mail*

> 'Read Mosley's, in many ways, excellent book. But read it critically.' **Edward Ingram**, *Philosophy Now*

£8.95/$17.90, 9780907845645 (pbk), *Societas* V.6

Off With Their Wigs!
Charles Banner and Alexander Deane

On June 12, 2003, a press release concerning a Cabinet reshuffle declared as a footnote that the ancient office of Lord Chancellor was to be abolished and that a new supreme court would replace the House of Lords as the highest appeal court. This book critically analyses the Government's proposals and looks at the various alternative models for appointing judges and for a new court of final appeal.

'A cogently argued critique.' *Commonwealth Lawyer*

£8.95/$17.90, 9780907845843 (pbk), *Societas* V.7

The Modernisation Imperative
Bruce Charlton & Peter Andras

Modernisation gets a bad press in the UK, and is blamed for increasing materialism, moral fragmentation, the dumbing-down of public life, declining educational standards, occupational insecurity and rampant managerialism. But modernisation is preferable to the likely alternative of lapsing back towards a 'medieval' world of static, hierarchical and coercive societies – the many and serious criticisms of modernisation should be seen as specific problems relating to a process that is broadly beneficial for most of the people, most of the time.

'A powerful and new analysis'. **Matt Ridley**

£8.95/$17.90, 9780907845522 (pbk), *Societas* V.8

Self and Society, *William Irwin Thompson*

£8.95/$17.90, 9780907845829 (pbk), *Societas* V.9
now superceded by Vol.41 (see above, p.S6)

The Party's Over
Keith Sutherland

This book questions the role of the party in the post-ideological age and concludes that government ministers should be appointed by headhunters and held to account by a parliament selected by lot.

'Sutherland's model of citizen's juries ought to have much greater appeal to progressive Britain.' *Observer*

'An extremely valuable contribution.' *Tribune*

'A political essay in the best tradition – shrewd, erudite, polemical, partisan, mischievous and highly topical.' *Contemporary Political Theory*

£8.95/$17.90, 9780907845515 (pbk), *Societas* V.10

Our Last Great Illusion

Rob Weatherill

This book aims to refute, primarily through the prism of modern psychoanalysis and postmodern theory, the notion of a return to nature, to holism, or to a pre-Cartesian ideal of harmony and integration. Far from helping people, therapy culture's utopian solutions may be a cynical distraction, creating delusions of hope. Yet solutions proliferate in the free market; this is why therapy is our last great illusion. The author is a psychoanalytic psychotherapist and lecturer, Trinity College, Dublin.

'Challenging, but well worth the engagement.' *Network*

£8.95/$17.90, 9780907845959 (pbk), *Societas* V.11

The Snake that Swallowed its Tail

Mark Garnett

Liberal values are the hallmark of a civilised society, but depend on an optimistic view of the human condition, Stripped of this essential ingredient, liberalism has become a hollow abstraction. Tracing its effects through the media, politics and the public services, the book argues that hollowed-out liberalism has helped to produce our present discontent.

'This arresting account will be read with profit by anyone interested in the role of ideas in politics.' **John Gray**, *New Statesman*

'A spirited polemic addressing the malaise of British politics.' **Michael Freeden**, *The European Legacy*

£8.95/$17.90, 9780907845881 (pbk), *Societas* V.12

Why the Mind is Not a Computer

Raymond Tallis

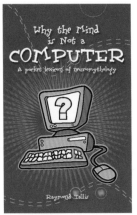

The equation 'Mind = Machine' is false. This pocket lexicon of 'neuromythology' shows why. Taking a series of keywords such as calculation, language, information and memory, Professor Tallis shows how their misuse has a misled a generation. First of all these words were used literally in the description of the human mind. Then computer scientists applied them metaphorically to the workings of machines. And finally the use of the terms was called as evidence of artificial intelligence in machines *and* the computational nature of thought.

'A splendid exception to the helpless specialisation of our age' **Mary Midgley**, *THES*

'A work of radical clarity.' *J. Consciousness Studies*

£8.95/$17.90, 9780907845942 (pbk), *Societas* V.13

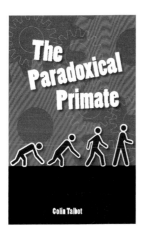

The Paradoxical Primate
Colin Talbot

This book seeks to explain how human beings can be so malleable, yet have an inherited set of instincts. When E.O. Wilson's *Consilience* made a plea for greater integration, it was assumed that the traffic would be from physical to human science. Talbot reverses this assumption and reviews some of the most innovative developments in evolutionary psychology, ethology and behavioural genetics.

> 'Talbot's ambition is admirable…a framework that can simultaneously encompass individualism and concern for collective wellbeing.' *Public* (The Guardian)

£8.95/$17.90, 9780907845850 (pbk), *Societas* V.14

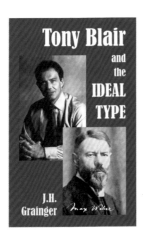

Tony Blair and the Ideal Type
J.H. Grainger

The 'ideal type' is Max Weber's hypothetical leading democratic politician, whom the author finds realized in Tony Blair. He is a politician emerging from no obvious mould, treading no well-beaten path to high office, and having few affinities of tone, character or style with his predecessors. He is the Outsider or Intruder, not belonging to the 'given' of British politics and dedicated to its transformation. (The principles outlined are also applicable. across the parties, in the post-Blair period.) The author was reader in political science at the Australian National University and is the author of *Character and Style in English Politics* (CUP).

> 'A brilliant essay.' **Simon Jenkins**, *Sunday Times*
> 'A scintillating case of the higher rudeness.' *Guardian*

£8.95/$17.90, 9781845400248 (pbk), *Societas* V.15

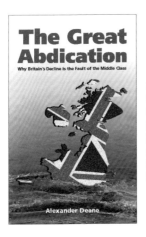

The Great Abdication
Alex Deane

According to Deane, Britain's middle class has abstained from its responsibility to uphold societal values, resulting in the collapse of our society's norms and standards. The middle classes must reinstate themselves as arbiters of morality, be unafraid to judge their fellow men, and follow through with the condemnation that follows when individuals sin against common values.

> '[Deane] thinks there is still an element in the population which has traditional middle-class values. Well, maybe.' **George Wedd**, *Contemporary Review*

£8.95/$17.90, 9780907845973 (pbk), *Societas* V.16

Neil MacCormick

Who's Afraid of a
European
Constitution?

Who's Afraid of a European Constitution?
Neil MacCormick

This book discusses how the EU Constitution was drafted, whether it promised any enhancement of democracy in the EU and whether it implied that the EU is becoming a superstate. The arguments are equally of interest regarding the EU Reform Treaty.

Sir Neil MacCormick is professor of public law at Edinburgh University. He was an MEP and a member of the Convention on the Future of Europe.

£8.95/$17.90, 9781845392 (pbk), *Societas* V.17

Darwinian Conservatism
Larry Arnhart

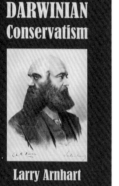

DARWINIAN
Conservatism

Larry Arnhart

The Left has traditionally assumed that human nature is so malleable, so perfectible, that it can be shaped in almost any direction. Conservatives object, arguing that social order arises not from rational planning but from the spontaneous order of instincts and habits. Darwinian biology sustains conservative social thought by showing how the human capacity for spontaneous order arises from social instincts and a moral sense shaped by natural selection. The author is professor of political science at Northern Illinois University.

'Strongly recommended.' *Salisbury Review*

'An excellent book.' **Anthony Flew**, *Right Now!*

'Conservative critics of Darwin ignore Arnhart at their own peril.' *Review of Politics*

96 pp., £8.95/$17.90, 9780907845997 (pbk.), *Societas,* Vol. 18

Doing Less With Less: Making Britain More Secure
Paul Robinson

Doing Less with Less
Making Britain More Secure

Paul Robinson

Notwithstanding the rhetoric of the 'war on terror', the world is now a far safer place. However, armed forces designed for the Cold War encourage global interference through pre-emption and other forms of military interventionism. We would be safer with less. The author, an ex-army officer, is assistant director of the Centre for Security Studies at Hull University.

'Robinson's criticisms need to be answered.'
Tim Garden, *RUSI Journal*

'The arguments in this thesis should be acknowledged by the MOD.' **Major General Patrick Cordingley DSO**

£8.95/$17.90, 9781845400422 (pbk), *Societas* V.19

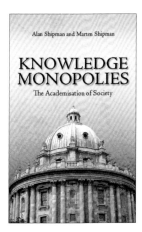

Knowledge Monopolies
Alan Shipman & Marten Shipman

Historians and sociologists chart the *consequences* of the expansion of knowledge; philosophers of science examine the *causes*. This book bridges the gap. The focus is on the paradox whereby, as the general public becomes better educated to live and work with knowledge, the 'academy' increases its intellectual distance, so that the nature of reality becomes more rather than less obscure.

'A deep and searching look at the successes and failures of higher education.' *Commonwealth Lawyer*

'A must read.' *Public* (The Guardian)

£8.95/$17.90, 9781845400286 (pbk), *Societas* V.20

The Referendum Roundabout
Kieron O'Hara

A lively and sharp critique of the role of the referendum in modern British politics. The 1975 vote on Europe is the lens to focus the subject, and the controversy over the referendum on the European constitution is also in the author's sights.

The author is a senior research fellow at the University of Southampton and author of *Plato and the Internet*, *Trust: From Socrates to Spin* and *After Blair: Conservatism Beyond Thatcher* (2005).

£8.95/$17.90, 9781845400408 (pbk), *Societas* V.21

The Moral Mind
Henry Haslam

The reality and validity of the moral sense took a battering in the last century. Materialist trends in philosophy, the decline in religious faith, and a loosening of traditional moral constraints added up to a shift in public attitudes, leaving many people aware of a questioning of moral claims and uneasy with a world that has no place for the morality. Haslam shows how important the moral sense is to the human personality and exposes the weakness in much current thinking that suggests otherwise.

'Marking a true advance in the discussion of evolutionary explanations of morality, this book is highly recommended for all collections.' **David Gordon**, *Library Journal*

'An extremely sensible little book. It says things that are really rather obvious, but which have somehow got forgotten.' **Mary Midgley**

£8.95/$17.90, 9781845400163 (pbk), *Societas* V.22

Putting Morality Back Into
Politics *Richard D. Ryder*

Ryder argues that the time has come for public policies to be seen to be based upon moral objectives. Politicians should be expected routinely to justify their policies with open moral argument. In Part I, Ryder sketches an overview of contemporary political philosophy as it relates to the moral basis for politics, and Part 2 suggests a way of putting morality back into politics, along with a clearer emphasis upon scientific evidence. Trained as a psychologist, the author has also been a political lobbyist, mostly in relation to animal welfare.

£8.95/$17.90, 9781845400477 (pbk), *Societas* V.23

Village Democracy
John Papworth

'A civilisation that genuinely reflects all that human beings long for and aspire to can only be created on the basis of each person's freely acknowledged power to decide on each of the many questions that affect his life.' In the forty years since he wrote those words in the first issue of his journal *Resurgence*, John Papworth has not wavered from that belief. This latest book passionately restates his argument for radical decentralisation.

'If we are to stand any chance of surviving we need to heed Papworth's call for decentralisation.'
Zac Goldsmith, *The Ecologist*

£8.95/$17.90, 9781845400644 (pbk), *Societas* V.24

Debating Humanism
Dolan Cummings (ed.)

Broadly speaking, the humanist tradition is one in which it is we as human beings who decide for ourselves what is best for us, and are responsible for shaping our own societies. For humanists, then, debate is all the more important, not least at a time when there is discussion about the unexpected return of religion as a political force. This collection of essays follows the Institute of Ideas' inaugural 2005 Battle of Ideas festival. Contributors include Josie Appleton, Simon Blackburn, Robert Brecher, Andrew Copson, Dylan Evans, Revd. Anthony Freeman, Frank Furedi, A.C. Grayling, Dennis Hayes, Elisabeth Lasch-Quinn, Kenan Malik and Daphne Patai.

£8.95/$17.90, 9781845400699 (pbk), *Societas* V.25

The Right Road to Radical Freedom *Tibor R. Machan*

This work focuses on the topic of free will – do we as individual human beings choose our conduct, at least partly independently, freely? He comes down on the side of libertarians who answer Yes, and scorns the compatibilism of philosophers like Daniel Dennett, who try to rescue some kind of freedom from a physically determined universe. From here he moves on to apply his belief in radical freedom to areas of life such as religion, politics, and morality, tackling subjects as diverse as taxation, private property, justice and the welfare state.

£8.95/$17.90, 9781845400187 (pbk), *Societas* V.26

Paradoxes of Power: Reflections on the Thatcher Interlude
Sir Alfred Sherman

In her memoirs Lady Thatcher herself pays tribute to her former adviser's 'brilliance', the 'force and clarity of his mind', his 'breadth of reading and his skills as a ruthless polemicist'. She credits him with a central role in her achievements. Born in 1919 in London's East End, until 1948 Sherman was a Communist and fought in the Spanish Civil War. But he ended up a free-market crusader.

'These reflections by Thatcherism's inventor are necessary reading.' **John Hoskyns**, *Salisbury Review*

£8.95/$17.90, 9781845400927 (pbk), *Societas* V.27

Public Health & Globalisation
Iain Brassington

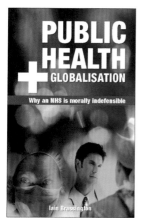

This book claims that the NHS is morally indefensible. There is a good moral case in favour of a *public* health service, but these arguments do not point towards a *national* health service, but to something that looks far more like a *transnational* health service. Drawing on Peter Singer's famous arguments in favour of a duty of rescue, the author argues that the cost of the NHS is unjustifiable. If we accept a duty to save lives when the required sacrifice is small, then we ought also to accept sacrifices in the NHS in favour of foreign aid. This does not imply that the NHS is wrong; just that it is wrong to spend large amounts on one person in Britain when we could save more lives elsewhere.

£8.95/$17.90, 9781845400798 (pbk), *Societas* V.28

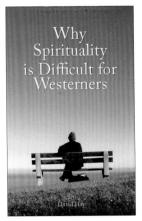

Why Spirituality is Difficult for Westerners *David Hay*

Zoologist David Hay holds that religious or spiritual awareness is biologically natural to the human species and has been selected for in organic evolution because it has survival value. Although naturalistic, this hypothesis is not intended to be reductionist. Indeed, it implies that all people have a spiritual life. This book describes the historical and economic context of European secularism, and considers recent developments in neurophysiology of the brain as it relates to religious experience.

£8.95/$17.90, 9781845400484 (pbk), *Societas* V.29

Earthy Realism: The Meaning of GAIA
Mary Midgley (ed.)

GAIA, named after the ancient Greek mother-goddess, is the notion that the Earth and the life on it form an active, self-maintaining whole. It has a *scientific* side, as shown by the new university departments of earth science which bring biology and geology together to study the continuity of the cycle. It also has a visionary or *spiritual* aspect. What the contributors to this book believe is needed is to bring these two angles together. With global warming now an accepted fact, the lessons of GAIA have never been more relevant and urgent. Foreword by James Lovelock.

£8.95/$17.90, 9781845400804 (pbk), *Societas* V.30

Joseph Conrad Today
Kieron O'Hara

This book argues that the novelist Joseph Conrad's work speaks directly to us in a way that none of his contemporaries can. Conrad's scepticism, pessimism, emphasis on the importance and fragility of community, and the difficulties of escaping our history are important tools for understanding the political world in which we live. He is prepared to face a future where progress is not inevitable, where actions have unintended consequences, and where we cannot know the contexts in which we act. The result can hardly be called a political programme, but Conrad's work is clearly suggestive of a sceptical conservatism of the sort described by the author in his 2005 book *After Blair: Conservatism Beyond Thatcher*.

£8.95/$17.90, 9781845400668 (pbk.), *Societas* V.31